The Creative Vision

THE
CREATIVE
VISION

Modern European

Writers On Their

Art ❋ *Edited By*

Haskell M. Block &

Herman Salinger

GROVE PRESS, INC. / NEW YORK

EVERGREEN BOOKS LTD. / LONDON

Preface

The Creative Vision is a collection of essays by major European literary figures of the twentieth century. In these essays, the writer discusses and interprets either his own writings or those of kindred spirits or the problems of the literary artist generally. In making our selections, we have limited ourselves to statements by writers on the subject of their art, in the hope that this book will provide not only pleasure, but direct illumination of some of the great novels, plays, and poems of our time. In this respect, *The Creative Vision* is not simply another collection of contemporary literary criticism, for only essays by active practitioners of the arts of poetry, drama, and fiction have been included. To have added contributions by writers who were primarily literary critics or aestheticians would have produced a different book, in large measure alien to our purpose.

In limiting our selections to continental European literature, we do not wish to imply any exclusiveness in taste or prejudice in editorial judgment. It would not have been difficult to augment the collection with similar selections from English and American writing as well as from less familiar literatures. Part of the value of this book lies in the fact that in it, several compositions of first-rate importance are made available in English for the first time. In some instances, the editors deliberately passed over better known and perhaps more characteristic essays because they are readily available in translation elsewhere and are familiar to students of modern literature. It must be added that in a very few instances, we were unable to obtain authorization to include writings which also deserve a place in this collection. On the positive side, it should be noted that not a few of the selections that make up our table of contents are difficult to find even in their original texts, and remain among their authors' fugitive and uncollected pieces. All of the translations in this volume, whether by the editors or not, have been carefully checked against the original texts. We have not hesitated to seek help in the preparation and revision of the versions here presented, but for whatever weaknesses they may have the editors accept full responsibility. Translation is at best an approximation and infallibility is the portion of gods, not of men. We have prepared this book in the hope that it will be instrumental in guiding its readers to a more intimate familiarity with the great European literature of our time.

The editors should like to express their gratitude to all who aided them in their task. We wish to record our keen sense of obligation to Mrs. Sylvia G. Goldfrank, Mrs. Charlotte Kohler, Mrs. Francesca Langbaum, Madame Gérard Mante-Proust, Dr. Gottfried Bermann Fischer, Dr. Moritz Hauptmann, Professor Philip Kolb, Monsieur Jean Lambert, Monsieur Dionys Mascolo, Mr. Jackson Mathews, Professor Eduardo Neale-Silva, Monsieur Jean Schlumberger, Avvocato Enzo Scipioni, and to our fellow translators whose names are indicated in the footnotes. We are especially grateful to Miss Marguerite A. Christensen of the University of Wisconsin Memorial Library for obtaining indispensable materials through inter-library loans, to Mrs. Mary E. Bakken for her tireless work in the preparation of the manuscript, and to Miss Judith Schmidt and Mr. Barney Rosset of Grove Press for their warm and generous help from the very beginning of our collaboration.

H.M.B.   *Madison, Wisconsin*
H.S.   *Durham, North Carolina*

Acknowledgments

The editors should like to thank all the copyright owners who granted permission to reprint the texts and translations in this collection. Full bibliographical references will be found in the footnotes to the essays.

We hereby acknowledge our appreciation and gratitude: To the Bollingen Foundation, New York, for permission to include "Poésie Pure" and "Au sujet du '*Cimetière marin*'" by Paul Valéry. To Insel-Verlag, Wiesbaden, for permission to include "Über den jungen Dichter" and "Ur-Geräusch" by Rainer Maria Rilke. To Hogarth Press, London, for permission to include the translation of Rainer Maria Rilke's "The Young Poet" by G. Craig Houston. To Carl Niemeyer for permission to include his translation of Rainer Maria Rilke's "Primal Sound." To the Comité d'Administration de l'Héritage Littéraire d'André Gide, for permission to include "A propos de la *Symphonie pastorale*" and "Paul Valéry" by André Gide. To Mercure de France, Paris, for permission to include "Paul Valéry" by André Gide. To John Lehmann for permission to include the translation of André Gide's "Paul Valéry" by Madame Dorothy Bussy. To Madame Gérard Mante-Proust for permission to include the remarks of Marcel Proust in an interview published in *Le Temps* (Paris), November 13, 1913. To Random House, Inc., New York, for permission to include a selection from *The Past Recaptured* by Marcel Proust, copyright 1932 by Random House, Inc. To S. Fischer Verlag, Frankfurt am Main, and to Frau Katja Mann for permission to include "Die Kunst des Romans" and "Der Künstler und die Gesellschaft" by Thomas Mann. To the Amministrazione degli Eredi di Luigi Pirandello for permission to include "Teatro e letteratura" and "Teatro nuovo e teatro vecchio" by Luigi

Pirandello. To Francisco García Lorca and New Directions for permission to include "Charla sobre teatro" by Federico García Lorca. To Editions Bernard Grasset, Paris, for permission to include "Discours sur le théâtre" and a selection from *Visitations* by Jean Giraudoux. To Jean Anouilh for permission to include his essay, "A Jean Giraudoux." To the *Tulane Drama Review* for permission to include the translation of Jean Anouilh's "To Jean Giraudoux" by Arthur Evans. To Suhrkamp Verlag, Berlin and Frankfurt am Main, for permission to include "Vergnügungstheater oder Lehrtheater?" and "Observations on *Mother Courage*" by Bertolt Brecht. To *Mainstream*, New York, for permission to include the translation of Bertolt Brecht's "Theatre for Pleasure or Theatre for Learning?" by Edith Anderson. To Librairie Gallimard, Paris, for permission to include a selection from *Esquisse d'une psychologie du cinéma* by André Malraux, and for permission to include "La Responsabilité de l'Ecrivain" and "Ecrire pour son époque" by Jean-Paul Sartre. To UNESCO, Paris, for permission to include the translation of Jean-Paul Sartre's "The Responsibility of the Writer" by Betty Askwith. To *The Virginia Quarterly Review*, Charlottesville, Va., for permission to include the translation of Jean-Paul Sartre's "We Write for Our Own Time" by Sylvia Glass. To Verlag der Arche Peter Schifferli, Zürich, for permission to include Friedrich Duerrenmatt's "Anmerkung" to *Der Besuch der Alten Dame* in his collection, *Komödien I*.

Contents

Introduction

The universal characteristic of twentieth-century European literature is its extreme self-consciousness. More than ever artistic creation has been at the same time a critical act, and more than ever writers have felt compelled to theorize about their art and to justify and elucidate their compositions. For virtually all the great writers of our time, the claims of critical intelligence have extended far beyond the limits of their own work, to embrace, not only the writings of their contemporaries, but also the whole of artistic experience. The essays collected in this book are decisive evidence of the dominance of critical intelligence in recent European literature. Any sharp distinction between critical and creative activity has all but fallen away.

If, on the one hand, the very existence of these essays is in itself of immense importance as a key to the character of modern literature, we should not forget that the act of self-examination, of meditation on the meaning of one's art, and of reflection on one's individual writings, has been a preoccupation of European writers for hundreds of years, pursued with varying degrees of intensity in various times and places. The very act of literary creation implies a selection, of theme, of form, of language, of innumerable minute particulars, that shape and define the work of art. In this sense, every writer is necessarily a critic and, in the act of composition, the greatest writers are those with the deepest, most comprehensive critical powers. Yet the insistence on critical elaboration, on the interpretation of one's own art, has never been more widespread than it is today.

Why this obsessive self-consciousness? Would not a writer's novels, poems, plays, carry their own explanation? How can we account for the dominance of the reflective mind in the world of artistic expression?

Perhaps the nearest explanation is to be found in the pervasive interest in questions of literary theory and literary interpretation on the part of the reading public of present-day Europe. Here, principles of aesthetics and criticism have an intimate bearing upon all of life—upon manners, morals, politics, friendship, love, hatred, and the whole realm of individual and collective experience. For the educated European, literature is a necessity of life, and literary values are readily and passionately converted into personal commitments. The contemporary European reading public demands that its writers engage in the discussion of their art, and, for the most part, the writers are quite willing to comply.

They are willing to comply with these demands because, as men of letters, it would not occur to them to do otherwise. Moreover, most writers are gratified by public interest in their work, and see in the preface, lecture, interview, article, or debate an opportunity to reciprocate this interest and to clarify the meaning of their art. Naturally, not all writers will participate with equal ardor in public meditation or self-scrutiny. Yet, in an age in which artists have suffered acutely from both physical and spiritual alienation, one may see in this fusion of the creative and critical act a deliberate reaching out for comprehension and communion.

If we consider the intense preoccupation with the reflective consciousness in literary creation which the Symbolists inherited from Edgar Allen Poe and which they in turn transmitted to our own age, we have yet another explanation for the modern writer's obsession with his art. The lucidity and conscious control which dominated the concept of the creative act in Symbolist aesthetics is but an extreme formulation of an awareness, common throughout literary history, of the deliberate character of artistic creation, even as a consequence of poetic inspiration. The absorption with the artist's ways and means is in this sense part of the endless struggle against the fortuitous that accompanies the act of organizing the brute inchoate substance of experience into a work of art.

From the heritage of Symbolism too has come the notion

that the great literature of our time must necessarily be difficult. A poetics founded on the superior existence of a transcendent and supernatural realm of value, made visible only through analogies and "correspondences," necessarily gives rise to a literature that is complex, richly allusive, conceptually private. The ever-deepening exploration of inward vision that has marked literature in the Symbolist tradition in the twentieth century has placed a burden of justification, if not of explanation, on writers whose rendering of mystical or spiritual or intensely emotional experience has forced them to create a new literary language. The problem of communication is especially acute at a time when traditional formal structures are being repudiated, and when experiment is too rapid and too far-reaching to be readily absorbed through existing categories of apprehension. Certainly, this condition marks a large area of thought and expression in the contemporary European scene. The writer has perforce become a guide to his work, not necessarily an infallible guide or the best guide—and the presence of irony is not to be wholly ruled out—but, for the most part, the writer as critic is a valuable and sometimes even an indispensable collaborator, whose statement of aims and intentions illuminates not only the history of the composition of his works and the nature of the creative vision, but the work itself in its finished and created form. In this way, he participates directly in shaping or modifying the transaction that takes place between the reader and the work of art.

Even a casual reading of these essays will suggest the immense value that this critical enterprise has had for the writer. It is paradoxical that in an age marked by professed dedication to impersonality in art, personal experiences and attitudes have constituted a central part of the raw material of artistic experience, and we do not need the example of Flaubert to learn that the insistence on impersonality is itself an assertion of personality. In interpreting his art, the writer may come to create it anew, may undergo again the process of grappling with his materials, shaping them to his purpose. Like the novels, plays, and poems which have revealed their creators as giants of modern literature, these essays too testify to the imperious claims of creation, and are as necessary to the artist as are the more direct pursuits of his art.

For the reader, however, the value of these acts of introspection must be something else. These essays should lead us back to their authors' great works with a new understanding and sympathy. Indeed, they are best read as an intimate part of our larger literary experience and, if we are at all receptive to this form of direct address and persuasion, they cannot be read otherwise. On page after page, we can find attitudes, values, even the very words themselves, that bring us back to the literature that issued from the same pen. To be sure, the student or lover of modern literature will gain far more from these pages than will the reader less familiar with recent European literary trends, but precisely because the direct application of thought to expression is present, implicitly if not openly, throughout this collection, it can serve as an excellent introduction to the controlling themes and purposes of those writers whose works continue to compel our attention and our admiration. These essays, then, situate their authors in relation to their time as well as to their individual works; not only do they reveal some of the most intimate secrets of their writings; they constitute a living testimony of what it meant to be a writer in the first half of the twentieth century.

In essays in reflective criticism, the line between autobiography and art is thin indeed, for the writer as critic cannot help revealing what is characteristic, not only of an individual work, but of all of his works that respond to the same pressures. Conversely, the qualities of the man emerge in bold relief in his meditations on his art: the nervous energy, sensitivity, psychological curiosity, dignity, and passion characteristic of the great writers of our time animate and transform their essays in criticism into imaginative expression, into art itself. The chief justification for these essays may well be that the knowledge and insight they give us is at the same time a pleasure commensurate with the richness of their themes and subjects. This knowledge and insight is not simply a matter of language and style, but rather an expression of the total artistic vision which individuates and defines the most powerful imaginative creations of our time, and in which the writer and his work are inseparable.

Yet he who writes on his own art must perforce embrace the art of others as well. Unquestionably, not a few of our writers would have made excellent professional critics had they chosen to follow this bent, and their broad formulations as well as their specific observations and judgments are of the keenest interest. Animated in large part by the profound impact of philosophy on literature, they have not hesitated to take on the role of the aesthetician, to concern themselves with general problems of artistic theory and to propound solutions that do far more than simply rationalize what they themsleves were doing in their literary endeavors. Long ago, philosophers and poets alike discovered that self-examination can be a source of general as well as of individual truths, of insight into the totality of experience as well as into local and particular circumstances. This is not to identify the reflective artist with the philosopher, for the artist aims, not at a complete and systematic explanation of the universe, but at the clarification of his art. What philosophical speculations we find in these essays are rooted in a concrete and empirical preoccupation with the artist's own techniques and processes. Nevertheless, this very concern may often lead to the formulation of aesthetic truths that are more commonly the product of rigorous philosophical examination.

A glance at some of the recurrent considerations in these essays might help to clarify the affinity between the artist and the aesthetician, who often arrive at a common meeting point from opposite directions. This convergence is especially evident in a pervasive concern with language, its residual properties, its capacities and operative powers, both in common discourse and in poetic expression, for words are the materials of the art of literature as well as of habitual communication. The reader interested in theory of language will find compelling evidence in virtually every essay in this collection, in Valéry and Rilke, Proust and Mann, Pirandello and García Lorca, Giraudoux and Sartre, of the preoccupation with language that extends over the length and breadth of recent European literature.

Other recurrent topics and *motifs* similarly point to the intimate alliance between aesthetics and art. The affinity of literature and the other arts—notably painting, music, and sculpture—is a major source of freedom and direction in the writer's pursuit of his vocation. Or again, the problem of structure, the formal organization of the parts of a work of art, the nature of the individual parts, the norms which define and control their interplay, are all matters as vital to the poet or playwright or novelist as they are to the aesthetician, and it is striking indeed to see how age-old theories of art are revived and modified in the writer's quest for the essential meaning of his work. Throughout these essays, the nature of the artist, the unique and individual qualities of his art, and the relation of that art to his audience, are interlocking preoccupations which help to confer on what might seem to be a random collection of personal reflections, a high degree of coherence and mutuality.

Of course, there are important differences as well, differences that can be explained not only by the diverse personalities whose work is here represented, but by the changing currents of literary expression of our time. No matter how we may evaluate contemporary literature, it should be clear in retrospect that the older writers of the present century were animated by a quest for the monumental that frequently led them to break openly with established forms and, at the same time, to enlarge the dimensions of their art to the plane of universal prophecy, altogether removed from the claims and restrictions of observable reality. The writers who came afterwards, more receptive to the demands of the topical and immediate, have been more modest in their themes and more limited in their innovations. Perhaps the appetite for the gigantic has been satisfied; or perhaps a period of consolidation must follow an era of intense and far-reaching formal experimentation. Even so, writers perpetually learn from other writers, and what the more recent writers in this collection share with their predecessors is far more important than what divides them.

For what they share we may in some measure share with them: the celebration of the creative life, the joy as well as the anguish of the artistic calling, the solitude and communion, the responsibility and freedom, the magic and wonder of the creative vision, the union of criticism and creation in an act of love.

The Creative Vision

Pure Poetry: NOTES FOR A LECTURE

PAUL VALÉRY

Today there is a good deal of excitement in the world (I mean in the world of the most precious and most useless things) over these two words: *pure poetry*. I am somewhat responsible for this excitement. A few years ago, in a preface to a friend's book of poems, I happened to express these words without attaching any extreme importance to them and without forseeing the conclusions that various persons concerned with poetry would draw from them. I knew quite well what I meant by those words, but I did not know that they would give rise to such reverberations and reactions among lovers of literature. I merely wanted to draw attention to a fact, and certainly not to set forth a theory or, worse yet, establish a doctrine and regard as heretics those who would not share it. To my mind, every written work, every product of language, contains certain fragments or recognizable elements endowed with properties that we will examine and which I will provisionally call *poetic*. Whenever speech exhibits *a certain deviation* from the most direct expression—that is, the most *insensible* expression of thought; whenever these deviations make us aware in some way of a world of relationships distinct from purely practical reality, we conceive more or less clearly of the possibility of enlarging this exceptional area, and we have the sensation of seizing the fragment of a noble and living substance which is perhaps capable of development and cultivation; and which, once developed and used, constitutes poetry in its artistic effect.

"Poésie Pure: Notes pour une Conférence" was first published in *Poësie, Essai sur la Poëtique et le Poëte*, Collection Bertrand Guégan, Paris, 1928. Valéry's notes were prepared for a lecture presented in December, 1927. Translated by Haskell M. Block.

Whether it is possible to make a work of art consisting wholly of these recognizable elements, so fully distinct from those of the language I have called *insensible*—whether it is possible, consequently, in a work written in verse or otherwise, to give the impression of a complete system of *reciprocal* relations between our images and ideas on the one hand and our means of expression on the other, a system which would correspond especially to the creation of an emotive state of mind—this, on the whole, is the problem of pure poetry. I mean *pure* in the way in which the doctor speaks of pure water. I mean that the question is to know if we can bring about a work which would be *pure* of elements that are not poetic. I have always held, and still do, that this is an unattainable object, and that poetry is always an effort to approach this purely ideal condition. In sum, what we call a *poem* is made up in practice of fragments of *pure poetry* inserted into the substance of a discourse. A very beautiful line is a very pure element of poetry. The banal comparison of a beautiful line to a diamond makes it clear that the feeling of this quality of purity is in every mind.

The inconvenience of this phrase, *pure poetry*, is that it makes one think of a moral purity which is not the issue here, for the idea of pure poetry is for me, quite the contrary, an essentially analytic idea. Pure poetry is, in sum, a fiction deduced from observation which should help us make precise our idea of poems in general and guide us in the difficult and important study of the diverse and multiform relations of language to the effects it produces on men. It would, perhaps, be much better instead of *pure poetry* to say *absolute poetry*, and we should then have to understand it as a search for the effects resulting from the relationships of words, or rather of the interrelations of their resonances, which suggests, in sum, *an exploration of the whole domain of the sensibility that is governed by language.* This exploration might be made gropingly, for such is the way it is generally done. But it is not impossible that it may one day be carried out systematically.

I have tried to construct and I am trying to give a clear idea of the poetic problem or, at least, what I believe to be a *clearer* idea of this problem. It is remarkable that these questions should today arouse a widespread interest. Never, it seems, has so large a public been concerned. We can be present at discussions, we can see experiments that are not restricted, as in times past, to narrow cliques and to a very small number of amateurs and experimenters; but more wonderful yet, in our age we see even in the public at large a kind of interest, sometimes impassioned, attach itself to these almost theological discussions. (What can be more theological than to debate, for example, on inspiration and labor, on the value of intuition and of the artifices of art? Have we not here problems altogether comparable to the famous theological problem of grace and works? Likewise, there are problems in poetry which, opposing the rules that have been determined and fixed by tradition and the immediate data of personal experience or of personal meaning, are absolutely analogous to the problems that are similarly found in the domain of theology, between the personal meaning, the direct knowledge of divine things, and the teachings of various religions, the texts of the Scriptures and dogmatic forms. . . .)

But I come to the subject now with the firm intention of saying nothing that is a matter of sheer assertion or the result of light speculation. Let us go back to this word, "poetry," and let us observe first of all that this beautiful name engenders two distinct orders of concepts. We speak of "poetry" and we speak of "a poem." We say of a scene, a situation, and sometimes of a person, that they are *poetic;* on the other hand, we also speak of *the art of poetry* and we say: "This poem is beautiful." But in the first case we are concerned with the evidence of a certain kind of feeling; everyone is familiar with this peculiar trembling comparable to our condition when we feel ourselves excited, enchanted, by the effect of certain events. This condition is entirely independent of any determinate work of art and results naturally and spontaneously from a certain accord between our inner disposition, physical and psychic, and the circumstances (real or ideal) which act on us. But on the other hand, when we say *the art of poetry* or when we speak of *a poem* we are concerned clearly with the means of bringing about a condition analogous to the preceding condition, of artificially producing this kind of feeling. And this is not all. The means which serve to bring about this condition must be those which belong to the properties and the mechanism of articulate language. The feeling which I spoke of can be brought about by things. It can also be brought about by means quite different from those of language, such as architecture, music, etc., but poetry properly named has as its essence the use of the devices of language. As for independent poetic feeling, let us observe that it is distinguished from other human feelings by a singular character, an admirable property: that it tends to give us the sense of an illusion or the illusion of a world (of a *world* in which events, images, beings, things, if they do resemble those which inhabit the ordinary world, are, on the other hand, inexplicably but intimately related to the whole of our sensibility). Known objects and beings are thus in some way —forgive the expression—*musicalized;* they have become harmonious and resonant, and as if *in tune* with our sensibility. Poetic experience defined in this way bears great similarities to the dream state, or at least to the condition produced in certain dreams. Dream, when we return to it through memory, makes us understand that our consciousness can be awakened or filled, and satisfied, by a whole range of productions that differ noticeably in their laws from ordinary productions of perception. But this emotive world that we can know at times through dream can not be entered or left at will. *It is enclosed in us and we are enclosed in it*, which means that we have no way of acting on it in order to modify it and that, on the other hand, it can not coexist with our great power of action over the external world. It appears and disappears capriciously, but man has done for it what he has done or tried to do for everything precious and perishable: he has sought for and has found the means of recreating this condition at will, of regaining it when he wishes, and finally, of artificially developing these natural products of his sentient being. In some sort of way he has managed to extract from nature and redeem from the blind movement of time these formations or constructions that are so uncertain; in this design he makes use of several devices which I have already mentioned. Now, among these means of producing a poetic world, of reproducing and enriching it, perhaps the most venerable and also the most complex and the most difficult to use is language.

At this point I must make you feel or understand to what extent the task of the poet in the modern age is a delicate one, and how many difficulties (of which, happily, he is not always aware) the poet encounters in his task. Language is a common and practical element; it is thereby necessarily a coarse instrument, for everyone handles and appropriates it according to his needs and tends to deform it according to his personality. Language, no matter how personal it may be or how close the way of thinking in words may be to our spirit, is nevertheless *of statistical origin* and has *purely practical ends.* Now the poet's problem must be *to derive from this practical instrument the means of creating a work essentially not practical.* As I have already told you, it is a matter, for him, of creating a world or an order of things, a system of relations, without any relationship to the practical order.

To make you understand all the difficulties of this task, I am going to *compare the poet's gifts with those of the musician.* How fortunate is the musician! The evolution of his art has given him an altogether privileged position for centuries. What does music consist of? The sense of hearing gives us *the universe of noises.* Our ear admits an infinite number of sensations that it receives in some kind of order and of which it can single out four distinct qualities. Now ancient observations and very old experiments have made it possible to deduce, from *the universe of noises,* the system or *the universe of sounds*—which are particularly simple and recognizable noises, particularly prone to form combinations, associations, whose structure, sequence, differences or resemblances are perceived by the ear, or rather by the understanding, as soon as they are produced. These elements are pure or are composed of pure—that is to say, recognizable—elements. They are sharply defined and—a very important point—the way has been found to produce them in a constant and identical manner by means of instruments which are, basically, true instruments of measure. A musical instrument is one that can be gauged and used in such a way that from given actions a given result can be uniformly obtained. And here we see the remarkable result of this organization of the province of hearing: as the world of sounds is quite separate from that of noises, and as our ear is also accustomed to distinguishing them clearly, it follows that *if a pure sound*—that is, a relatively exceptional sound—*happens to be heard, at once a particular atmosphere is created, a particular state of expectation is produced in our senses, and this expectation tends,* to some degree, *to give rise to sensations of the same kind, of the same purity as the sensation produced.* If a pure sound is produced in a concert hall, *everything is changed within us;* we await the production of music. If, on the contrary, the reverse is tried; if during the performance of a composition in a concert hall a noise should be heard (a falling chair, the voice or cough of a listener), at once we feel that something inside us has been broken, there has been a violation of some sort of substance or law of association; *a universe is shattered,* a charm is wiped out.

Thus for the musician, before he has begun his work, all is in readiness so that the operation of his creative spirit may find, right from the start, the appropriate matter and means, without any possibility of error. He will not have to make this matter and means submit to any modification; he need only assemble elements which are clearly defined and ready-made.

But in how different a situation is the poet! Before him is ordinary language, this aggregate of means which are not suited to his purpose, not made for him. There have not been physicians to determine the relationships of these means for him; there have not been constructors of scales; no diapason, no metronome, no certitude of this kind. He has nothing but the coarse instrument of the dictionary and the grammar. Moreover, he must address himself not to a special and unique sense like *hearing*, which the musician bends to his will, and which is, besides, the organ *par excellence* of expectation and attention; but rather to a general and diffused expectation, and he does so through a language which is a very odd mixture of incoherent *stimuli*. Nothing is more complex, more difficult to make out, than the strange combination of qualities that exists in language. Everyone knows quite well how rare indeed are the agreements *of sound and sense;* and moreover, we all know that a discourse can develop qualities altogether different. A discourse can be logical and completely void of harmony; it can be harmonious and insignificant: it can be clear and lacking in any sort of beauty; it can be prose or poetry; and it is enough, to sum up all of these independent modes, to mention the various sciences which have been created to exploit this diversity of language and to study it under different aspects. Language is subject, in turn, to *phonetics,* along with *metrics* and *rhythm;* it has a *logical* aspect and a *semantic* aspect; it includes *rhetoric* and *syntax.* We know that all these diverse disciplines can be brought to bear on the same text in many mutually exclusive ways. . . . Here we have the poet come to grips with this ensemble so diverse and so rich in initial capacities; too rich, in sum, not to be confused. It is from it that he must draw his *art object,* the contrivance to produce poetic emotion—that is, he must force the practical instrument, the coarse instrument created by anyone at all, the instrument of every moment, used for immediate needs and modified at every instant by the living, to become, for the time that his attention gives to the poem, the substance of a selected emotive condition, quite distinct from all of the accidental conditions of indeterminate length which make up ordinary sensory or psychic existence. We can say without exaggeration that the common language is the fruit of the disorder of common life, because men of every sort, subject to an innumerable quantity of conditions and needs, receive it and make use of it as best they can for their desires and their interests so as to make possible relations between them; while the language of the poet, although he necessarily makes use of the elements furnished by this statistical disorder, constitutes, on the contrary, *an effort of man in isolation* to create an artificial and ideal order by means of a substance of vulgar origin.

If this paradoxical problem could be wholly resolved; that is, if the poet could manage to construct works where nothing that partakes of prose would be present—poems where the musical continuity would never be interrupted, where the relationships of meanings would be themselves forever like harmonic relations, *where the transmutation of thoughts from one into the other would be more important than any thought,* where the play of figures would contain the reality of the subject—then we could talk about *pure poetry* as though it existed. Such is not the case: the practical or pragmatic part of language, the logical habits and forms and, as I have indicated, the disorder, the irrationality that we find in the vocabulary (because of infinitely various derivations from very different ages in which the elements of the language were introduced) make the existence of these creations of absolute poetry impossible; but it is easy to conceive that the notion of such an ideal or imaginary condition is very precious for the appreciation of all observable poetry.

The conception of pure poetry is one of an inaccessible kind, of an ideal limit of the desires, the efforts, and the powers of the poet. . . .

Concerning Le Cimetière marin

PAUL VALÉRY

I do not know if it is still the custom to compose poems slowly, to hold them for many years between being and not-being, suspended before desire; to cultivate doubt, scruple, and regrets, so that a work of art, constantly taken up again and remade, gradually takes on the secret importance of an enterprise in the remaking of one's self.

Forty years ago this way of producing little was not unusual with poets and with some writers of prose. Time did not matter to them—a rather sublime point of view. Neither the Idol of the Beautiful nor the superstition of literary Eternity had yet been ruined, and the belief in Posterity was not altogether destroyed. There was a sort of *Ethic of Form* which led to infinite labor. Those who dedicated themselves to it knew well that the greater the effort, the smaller the number of persons who recognize and appreciate it. They toiled for a very few, and like saints. . . .

In this way, the "natural" or naive conditions for producing Literature became remote, and the composition of a product of the mind, which is *finite*, came little by little to be confused with the life of the mind itself—which is an endlessly operating power of transformation. Work came to matter for its own sake. In the eyes of such lovers of restlessness and perfection, a work of art is never *finished*—a word that had no meaning for them—but *abandoned*; and this abandonment, whether to the flames or to the public (and whether the result of fatigue or obligation), is for them a kind of *accident*, comparable to the interruption of a

This essay was first published as the Preface to Gustave Cohen, *Essai d'explication du "Cimetière marin,"* Librairie Gallimard, Paris, 1933, pp. 7-33. Translated by Haskell M. Block.

train of thought which fatigue, annoyance, or some external event happens to obliterate.

I had contracted this disease, this perverse delight in endless reworking, and this pleasure in the reversibility of works of art, at the critical age when the intellectual man is formed and fixed. I came upon them again in all their vigor when, nearing the age of fifty, circumstances happened to set me once again to writing poetry. Thus, I have lived a good deal with my poems. For almost ten years they were for me an occupation of indefinite duration—an exercise rather than an action, a quest rather than a fulfillment, a maneuver of myself by myself rather than preparation with the public in view. I believe they have taught me more things than one.

All the same, I do not advise others to adopt this system. I am not qualified to give anyone else the least bit of advice, and besides, I doubt that my advice would suit the young men of an age that is hurried, confused, and lacking in perspective. We are in a fog bank. . . .

If I have spoken of this long intimacy between a work of art and a "self," it was only in order to give an idea of the very strange feeling I experienced, one morning, at the Sorbonne, while listening to Professor Gustave Cohen explain "*Le Cimetière marin*" from the lecture platform.

My writings have never lacked commentaries, and I certainly cannot complain of any silence about them. I am accustomed to being elucidated, dissected, impoverished, enriched, exalted, and destroyed, to the point of no longer knowing *what* I was or *who* was being discussed; but reading what has been said about you is nothing alongside this strange sensation of hearing yourself discussed at the University, in the lecture hall, very much like a dead author.

In my time, living writers did not exist in the classroom, but it does not seem to me altogether bad that this is no longer the case.

30

The teaching of literature thus gains what the teaching of history might gain from an analysis of the present; I mean the intimation or the sense of those *forces* which give rise to events and forms. The past is only the *residence* of forms without forces; it is for us to supply it with life and necessity, and to ascribe to it our passions and our values.

I felt like my *Shadow*. . . . I felt like a captured shadow, and yet, I identified myself from time to time with one or another of the students who were following the discussion, taking notes, and, now and then, turning to smile at this shadow whose poem their teacher read and commented on, stanza by stanza. . . .

I must admit that *as a student*, I had little respect for the poet —isolated, exposed, and uncomfortable in his seat. My presence was strangely divided among several ways of being there.

Among the diversity of sensations and reflections that constituted for me that hour at the Sorbonne, dominant was the sense of contrast between the memory of my labor, which came back to me, and the finished shape, the fixed and determinate work of art to which Gustave Cohen's exegesis and analysis applied. It made me feel how our *being* is opposed to our *seeming*. On the one hand, my poem studied as a completed object, revealing to the examination of the expert its composition, its intentions, its means of action, its place in the system of literary history, its ties, and the probable condition of its author's mind. . . . On the other hand, the memory of my attempts, of my gropings, of my inner decipherings, of those very imperious verbal illuminations which suddenly impose a certain combination of words—as if, I was about to say, a particular grouping possessed some sort of intrinsic power. . . . I know not what *will* to come into being, altogether opposed to the "freedom" or the chaos of the mind, and which sometimes can keep the mind from deviating from its plan, and the poem from being quite different from what it was going to be and from what one thought it had to be. (You can see from this that the notion of an *Author* is not a simple one: it is only so when seen from the outside.)

While listening to Monsieur Cohen reading the stanzas of my text and giving to each its definite meaning and its particular value in the development of the whole, I was torn between the satisfaction of seeing that the intentions and expressions of a poem reputed to be most obscure were here understood and set forth perfectly well, and the odd, almost painful feeling to which I have just alluded. I will try to explain it briefly, so as to complete the commentary on a given poem considered as a *fact*, by a view of the circumstances which accompanied the birth of this poem, or of what it had been in the stage of desire and insistence within me.

Besides, I intervene only in order to introduce, for the sake (or by the subterfuge) of a particular instance, a few observations on the relations of a poet to his poem.

I must first state that *"Le Cimetière marin," such as it is*, is *for me* the result of the *interruption* of an inner effort by a chance event. One afternoon in 1920, our late lamented friend Jacques Rivière came to visit me, and found me at a "stage" of this *"Cimetière marin,"* thinking of reworking, cutting, substituting, interposing here and there. . . .

He would not leave me alone until he had got hold of it to read and, having read it, he carried it off. Nothing is more decisive than the mind of an editor of a literary magazine.

Thus, it was *by accident* that the shape of this work was fixed. I had absolutely nothing to do with it. Furthermore, I can never go over anything I have written without thinking that I would have done something quite different with it if some outside interruption or mere circumstance had not broken the enchantment of never finishing it. I like only the effort of work: beginnings bother me, and I suspect anything that comes at a single stroke to be capable of improvement. The spontaneous, even when it is excellent, even when it is attractive, has never seemed to me sufficiently *mine*. I do not say that I am right in this; I say that this is how I am. . . . The notion of an Author is no simpler than that of the Self: one additional degree of consciousness opposes a new *Same* to a new *Different*.

Literature, then, interests me *deeply* only to the extent that it engages the mind in certain transformations—those in which the exciting properties of language play a leading role. To be sure, I can pick up a book, read it and reread it with pleasure; but it does not possess me deeply unless I find in it the marks of thought *equal in power to that of language itself*. The ability to bend the common verb to unexpected results without breaking the "established forms"; the capture and subjection of things difficult to state; and especially the simultaneous control of syntax, harmony, and ideas (which is the problem of the purest poetry) are in my eyes the supreme aims of our art.

It may be that this way of feeling is shocking. It makes of "creation" a means. It leads to excesses. What is more, it tends to corrupt the naive pleasure of *belief*, which gives rise to the naive pleasure of creating, and which sustains all reading.

If the author knows himself a little too well, if the reader bestirs himself, what happens to pleasure, what happens to Literature?

This wayward venture into the difficulties that can arise between the "consciousness of self" and the habit of writing will certainly explain certain *inclinations* for which I have been criticized at times. For example, I have been reproached for giving out several versions of the same poem, even contradictory ones. I find this criticism quite unintelligible, as may well be expected from what I have just said. Quite the contrary, I should be tempted (if I followed my feeling) to urge poets to produce,

33

in the style of composers, a diversity of variations or solutions of the same subject. Nothing would seem to me to conform more closely to the idea I like to hold of a poet and of poetry.

The poet, to my mind, is recognized by his idols and his liberties, which are not those of most men. Poetry is different from prose in not having either the same inconvenience or the same freedoms. The essence of prose is to perish—that is, to be "understood," to be dissolved, destroyed once and for all, wholly replaced by the image or impulse that it signifies, according to the convention of language. For prose always assumes the universe of experience and acts, the universe in which—or *by dint of the grace of which*—our perceptions and our actions or feelings must ultimately correspond with one another or respond to one another in a single way: *uniformly*. The practical universe is reduced to a totality of *ends*. When a given end is attained, the word dies. This universe excludes ambiguity, eliminates it; it demands procedure by the shortest routes, and it stifles at once the harmonic relationships of each event generated in the mind.

But poetry demands or suggests a "Universe" that is quite different: a universe of reciprocal relations, analogous to the universe of sounds, in which musical thought arises and moves. In this poetic universe, resonance triumphs over causality, and the "form," far from dissolving into its effect, is as it were *reinvoked* by it. The Idea reclaims its voice.

(There results from all this an *enormous* difference between the constructive moments of prose and the creative moments of poetry.)

Thus, in the art of the Dance, as the condition of the dancer (or of the lover of ballets) is the object of this art, the movements and displacements of the body have no limit in *space*—no visible end; *nothing* which joins them cancels them out; and it never occurs to anyone to impose on choreographic movements the law of acts which are *nonpoetic* but *useful,* to be performed *with the greatest economy of effort,* and *by the shortest means.*

This comparison may serve to indicate that neither simplicity nor clarity are absolutes in poetry, where it is perfectly *reasonable*—and even necessary—to hold oneself in a condition as far removed as possible from that of prose, suffering the loss (without too many regrets) of as many readers as one must.

Voltaire, wonderfully, said that "Poetry is made only of beautiful details." I do not put it differently. The poetic universe of which I was speaking introduces itself through the number or, rather, by the density of images, figures, consonances, dissonances, by the enchainment of turns and rhythms—the essential being to avoid constantly whatever might lead back to prose, either by causing it to be missed, or by following nothing but the *idea.* . . .

In sum, the more a poem conforms to Poetry, the less it can be thought in prose without perishing. To summarize a poem, to put it in prose, is quite simply to misunderstand the essence of an art. Poetic necessity is inseparable from sensory form, and the thoughts set forth or suggested by a poetic text are in no way the unique and primary concern of discourse, but are rather the *means* which move together *equally* with the sounds, the cadences, the meter, and the embellishments, to provoke, to sustain a particular tension or exaltation, to produce in us a *world*—or a *mode of existence*—altogether harmonious.

Thus, if someone asks me, if someone wonders (as in fact happens, and sometimes rather acutely) what I "wanted to say" in a certain poem, I reply that I did not *want to say* but *wanted to do,* and it was the intention of *doing* which *made the meaning* of what I said. . . .

As for "*Le Cimetière marin,*" this intention at first was only a rhythmic form, empty, or filled with empty syllables, which happened to obsess me for a while. I noted that this form was de-casyllabic, and I reflected somewhat on this type so seldom used in modern poetry; it seemed poor and monotonous. It was slight indeed alongside the alexandrine, which three or four genera-tions of great artists prodigiously elaborated. The demon of generalization suggested that I try to raise this *Ten* to the power of *Twelve*. It proposed to me a particular stanza of six lines and the idea of a *composition* based on the number of these stanzas, and determined by a variety of tones and functions to be as-signed them. Between these stanzas, contrasts or correspondences were to be set up. This last condition soon demanded that the possible poem be a monologue of "myself," in which the simplest and most constant themes of my affective and intellectual life—just as they had imposed themselves on my adolescence and associated with the sea and the light at a certain place on the shores of the Mediterranean—were to be called forth, interwoven, contrasted. . . .

All this led to death and touched on pure thought. (The chosen line of ten syllables has some relation to Dante's line.)

My line had to be dense and strongly rhythmic. I knew that I was moving toward a monologue as personal, but also as uni-versal, as I could make it. The kind of line chosen, the form adopted for the stanzas, gave me conditions which favored cer-tain "movements," permitted certain changes in tone, evoked a certain style. . . . "*Le Cimetière marin*" was *conceived*. A rather long labor followed.

Whenever I think of the art of writing (in verse or in prose), the same "ideal" presents itself to my mind. The myth of "crea-tion" entices us to want to make something out of nothing. I like to think, then, that I find my work developing progressively out of pure conditions of form, more and more reflective—made precise to the point where they propose or virtually impose . . . a *subject*—or at least, a family of subjects.

Let us observe that precise conditions of form are nothing but the expression of intelligence and of the awareness that we have *means* at our disposition, and of their range as well as their limits and their defects. This is why I have on occasion defined the *writer* as a relationship between a certain "mind" and Language. . . .

But I know how fanciful is my "Ideal." The nature of language lends itself least of all to sustained combinations; and besides, the formation and habits of the modern reader, whose habitual diet of incoherence and violent effects makes all refinement of structure imperceptible to him, would hardly urge him to lose his way so far. . . .

Nevertheless, the very thought of constructions of this sort remains for me the most *poetic* of ideas: the idea of composition.

On this word I must stop. . . . It would lead me into all sorts of lengthy explanations. Nothing on the part of poets has more surprised and distressed me than the lack of complexity in their compositions. In the most famous lyrics, I find hardly more than purely linear developments—or . . . delirious ones—I mean, which move from place to place, with no more sequential organization than a trail of burning gunpowder. (I am not referring to poems in which a narrative dominates and the chronology of events intervenes: these are mixed works; operas, and not sonatas or symphonies.)

But my surprise lasted only long enough to remind me of my own experiments and of the almost hopeless difficulties I encountered in my attempts to *compose* in the lyric form. For here, detail is of essential importance at every moment, and the most beautiful and most learned foresight must compose with the uncertainty of happy chance. In the lyric universe, each moment must complete an indefinable alliance of the sensuous and the meaningful. The consequence is that the composition is, in some way, continuous, and can hardly fix itself in any time other than that of execution. There is not one time for the "substance" and another time for the "form"; and composition in this genre contrasts not only with disorder or disproportion, but with *decompo-*

sition. If the meaning and the sound (or the substance and the form) can easily dissociate themselves, the poem *decomposes.*

What follows from this is of first importance: the "ideas" which are present in a poetic work do not play the same part, are in no way *values of the same kind,* as "ideas" in prose.

I have said that *"Le Cimetière marin"* first came to my mind as a composition of stanzas of six ten-syllable lines. This decision enabled me to distribute rather easily in my work what it needed of the sensuous, affective, and abstract in order to suggest, transported into the poetic universe, the meditation of a certain *self.*

The need to produce contrasts and to maintain a kind of balance between the moments of this *self* led me (for example) to introduce at one point some recollection of philosophy. The lines in which the famous arguments of Zeno of Elea appear (but enlivened, intermixed, carried away with the violence of all dialectic, like a whole rigging by a sudden gust of wind) have the function of compensating, by a metaphysical tonality, for the sensual and the "too human" of the preceding stanzas; they also characterize more exactly *the person speaking*—a lover of abstractions; finally, they oppose to what was speculative and too attentive in him the present power of reflex whose sudden movement breaks up and dissipates a state of somber fixity, as a complement to the reigning splendor, at the same time that it overturns a totality of *judgments* on everything human, inhuman, and superhuman. I corrupted the images of Zeno to express the rebellion against the duration and the acuteness of a meditation that makes one feel too cruelly the gap between *being* and *knowing* developed by the consciousness of consciousness. The *soul* naively wants to exhaust the infinite of the Eleatic.

But all I meant to take from philosophy was a little of its *color.*

The various preceding statements can give an idea of the reflections of a writer in the presence of a commentary on his work. He sees in it what it ought to have been, and what it could have been, much more than what it is. What, then, could interest him more than the result of a careful examination and the impressions of another's observation? It is not within me that the true unity of my work comes about. I have written a "score" —but I can hear it only when performed by the soul and the mind of someone else.

This is why Gustave Cohen's effort (not including the things in it which are much too kind to me) is particularly dear to me. He has sought out my intentions with remarkable care and method; he has applied to a contemporary text the same knowledge and the same precision which he is accustomed to show in his learned studies in literary history. He has outlined the architecture of this poem as well as indicated its detail—pointed out, for example, those recurrent phrases which reveal the inclinations, the characteristic repetitions of a mind. (There are some words which ring within us among all the others, like overtones of our deepest nature. . . .) To conclude, I am very grateful to him for having explained me so lucidly to his young students.

As for the *literal* interpretation, I have already set forth elsewhere my conviction on this subject; but it cannot be emphasized often enough; *there is no true meaning of a text.* The author has absolutely no authority. Whatever he *wanted to say,* he has written what he has written. Once published, a text is like a mechanism which everyone can use according to his ways and means: there is no certainty of its maker using it better than anyone else. Furthermore, if he really knows what he wanted to do, this knowledge always disturbs his perception of what he has done.

The Young Poet: (SOME CONJECTURES CONCERNING THE COMING INTO BEING OF POEMS)

RAINER MARIA RILKE

Still hesitating to distinguish between the predominant and the lesser among treasured experiences, I am confined to quite provisional means of expression when I attempt to describe the nature of a poet: that tremendous and childlike nature, which occurred (we do not understand how) not only in unsurpassably great figures of earlier times, but which is here also, beside us, actually mobilizing, it may be, in the boy who lifts up his great eyes and does not see us, this nature which assails young hearts, at a time when they are still powerless to face the slightest form of life, in order to fill them with capacities and relationships, which immediately exceed all that can be acquired in a whole existence; indeed, who would be able to speak calmly of this nature? Were it the case, that it did not occur any longer, that we could contemplate it at a distance in that improbable phenomenon, the poems of Homer: we should gradually formulate it, we should give to it a name and period, like the other things of the past; for what is it but the past that breaks out in the hearts which are convulsed by such forces? Here in our midst, in this multifariously modern city, in that honestly busy house, among the noise of vehicles and factories and the shouts of sellers of newspapers, capacious journals filled to the brim with events, suddenly, who knows, all the effort, all the urgency, all the energy are outweighed by the appearance of the Titans in a heart still

"Über den jungen Dichter" was written in 1913 and is included in Rilke's *Ausgewählte Werke*, Insel-Verlag, Leipzig, 1938, Vol. II, pp. 281-289. Translated by G. Craig Houston in Rainer Maria Rilke, *Selected Works, Vol. I: Prose*, The Hogarth Press, London, 1954, pp. 57-63. Revised by the editors.

immature. Nothing vouches for it but the coldness of a boy's hand; nothing but an upward glance terrifiedly withdrawn; nothing but the indifference of this young creature, who does not talk to his brothers and who rises, as soon as he can, from meals which expose him far too long to the judgment of his family. He scarcely knows whether he still belongs to his mother: so greatly have all the proportions of his feeling altered since the irruption of the elements into his infinite heart.

O you mothers of poets, you chosen resorts of the Gods, in whose womb even the unheard-of must have been agreed upon. Did you hear voices in the depth of your conception, or did the Heavenly Presences communicate only by signs?

I do not know how one can deny the utter wonderfulness of a world, in which the increase of what is known has never even approached the supply, which passes beyond all calculation. It is true, the gods have neglected no opportunity of exposing us: they let us uncover the great kings of Egypt in their tombs, and we were able to behold them in their natural corruption, to see how they were spared nothing. All the utmost achievements of these edifices and paintings led to nothing; the heavens did not become more serene behind the smoke of the balsam cooking, nor, apparently, did any company of the underworld make use of the loaves of clay and the concubines. Whosoever considers what wealth of purest and most tremendous ideas have here (and repeatedly) been rejected and repudiated by the incomprehensible Beings to whom they have been applied, how could he avoid trembling for our greater future? But let him consider, also, what the human heart would be, if certainty occurred at any place outside of it in all the world: ultimate certainty. How it would lose, at one blow, the tension it had developed through thousands of years, how it would remain a place worthy of praise, indeed, but one of which men would secretly tell, what it had been in former times. For truly, even the greatness of the gods depends upon their need: upon the fact that, whatever shrines may be kept for them, they are nowhere safe but in our heart. Into it they often plunge out of their sleep with their still confused plans; there they foregather, earnestly counseling; there their decree is irresistible.

What do all disillusionments prove, all unsatisfied burial chambers, all despoiled temples, if here, beside me, God becomes conscious of himself within a youth suddenly grown gloomy?

His parents see no future for him, his teachers think they have the clue to his unhappiness, his own mind renders the world vague to him, and his death keeps trying to find out the spot where he could be most easily broken: but so great is the carelessness of the heavenly power that it pours its waters into this undependable vessel. An hour since, the most fleeting glance of his mother could comprehend his nature; now she would be unable to gauge it, even though she included both resurrection and the fall of angels.

But what can a new creature do, that scarcely yet knows his own hands, without experience of his own nature, a stranger among the most ordinary turns of his mind, when he feels such an unheard of presence? How is he, who is obviously destined to be of a most precise nature later, to achieve his development between threats and caresses, both of which exceed the utmost effort of his unprepared powers? And it is not only that the bursting forth of greatness within him makes the heroic landscape of his feeling almost impassable to him: in proportion as his nature takes control there, in like measure, when he looks up, is he aware of mistrustful questions, bitter demands, and curiosity in the faces he had hitherto loved in all security. In such a situation a boy might surely always go away, go forth, and be a shepherd. He might, in long speechless days and nights, enrich his confused inner world with space wonderingly experienced; he might raise the crowded images in his soul to parity with the outspread stars. Oh, if only no one would try to persuade him and no one contradict him. Do you really wish to occupy the attention of *such* a one, one who is preoccupied beyond measure, prematurely occupied with an unfathomable nature?

Can we explain how he exists? The power which suddenly

inhabits him finds converse and kinship in the childhood that still lingers in every corner of his heart; and now we see toward what tremendous relationships this outwardly so inadequate condition lies open. This spirit so disproportionate in its dimensions, which has no room in the consciousness of the youth, hovers there above a developed underworld full of joys and terrors. From here alone, irrespective of the whole invisible-external creation, can it carry out its mighty purposes. But already it is tempted, by the pure communication of the senses of him whom it inhabits, to have dealings with the present world. And just as inwardly it finds its contact with the mightiest of hidden forces, so in things visible it is quickly and accurately served by small beckoning occasions; after all, it would be incompatible with the reticence of Nature to waken in the initiate what is truly significant otherwise than unobtrusively.

Whoever reads the early letters of Kleist will, according to the measure in which he understands that phenomenon, clarifying itself in thunderstorms, find the passage not unimportant which describes the arch of a certain gateway in Würzburg, one of the most timely impressions, on touching which genius, already tense, breaks out. Any thoughtful reader of Stifter (to give another example) could bring himself to imagine that the inner vocation of this poetic narrator became inevitable at that moment when he first attempted, on one unforgettable day, to bring nearer to him, by means of a telescope, some far-distant spot in the landscape, and then experienced within his utterly surprised vision a flight of spaces, of clouds, of objects, a shock of such richness that within these seconds his spirit, openly taken by surprise, received World as Danaë received the outpoured Zeus.

Ultimately, all poetic resolution may have realized itself unexpectedly by just such incidental causes, not only when it took possession of a temperament for the first time, but repeatedly, at every turn of a nature which was fulfilling itself artistically.

Who can name you all, you accomplices of inspiration, you who are no more than sounds or bells that cease, or strangely new bird voices in the neglected woods, or shining light thrown by an

opening window out into the hovering morning; or cascading
water; or air; or glances. Chance glances of passers-by, upward
glances of women sewing by the window, down to the unspeak-
ably troubled looking-about-them of crouching, anxious dogs,
so close to the expression of the schoolchildren. What agreed
purpose of calling forth greatness moves through the most triv-
ially commonplace! Events, so indifferent that they would not
be capable of deflecting the most yielding of destinies by a ten-
thousandth degree—behold: they beckon here, and the divine
line passes over them into the eternal.

The poet, with increasing insight into his limitless tasks, will
undoubtedly attach himself to what is greatest; where he finds it,
it will delight or humble him, according to his choice. But the
signal for the uprising in his heart will be given willingly by a
messenger who does not know what he is doing. It is unthinkable
that the poet should regulate himself from the very start by what
is great, since he is, indeed, destined to reveal himself through it,
his ever present goal, by ways still indescribably peculiar to him.
And how should it really have first become known to him, since
it was present in his original surroundings, masked perhaps, dis-
guising itself, or scorned, like the saint living in the intervening
space under the stairs? But if it once lay before him, openly
revealed, in its assured glory which is indifferent to us, would
he not then, like Petrarch, be compelled, at the sight of the countless vistas seen from the mountain he had climbed, to flee back
to the ravines of his own soul, which are of inexpressibly greater
concern to him, although he will never explore their depths, than
that foreign region which might, at need, be explored?

Alarmed within by the distant thunder of the god, bewildered
from without by an irresistible excess of phenomena, the object
of such violent treatment has only just room to stand on the narrow space between two worlds, until suddenly a neutral little
event inundates his monstrous condition with innocence. This is
the moment which places the great poem in the scales, in the one
tray of which there rests his heart, overburdened with infinite
responsibilities, the great poem producing the sublimely tran-
quilized balance.

44

The great poem. As I say it, it becomes clear to me that I have accepted it, until quite recently, as something which certainly exists, putting it highhandedly beyond any suspicion of coming into being. Even if the originator were to appear from behind it, I should not be able to imagine the power which all *at once* had broken so great a silence. Just as the builders of the cathedrals shot up, like grains of seed, immediately and without residue, into growth and blossom in their work, which stood there as if it had always been, no longer explicable as deriving from them: so the great poets of the past and the present remain entirely incomprehensible to me, the place of each being taken by the tower and bell of his heart. Only since a most proximate younger generation, striving upward and into the future, has embodied, not insignificantly, their own growth in the growth of their poems, does my eye seek to recognize, alongside of their achievement, the circumstances of the creative personality. But even now, when I must acknowledge that poems are formed, I am far from thinking them invented; it seems to me rather as if there appeared in the soul of the poetically inspired a spiritual predisposition, which was already present between us (like an undiscovered constellation).

If we consider what admirable achievement even now stands surety for some of those who have recently entered upon their thirties, we might almost hope that they would soon, by the finished quality of their work, make everything which in the last thirty years has called forth our admiration appear but the preparation for the fulfillment which their work achieves. It is clear that the most diverse circumstances must combine favorably, if such a resolute achievement is to be possible. If we examine these circumstances, the outward ones are so numerous, that in the end we give up the attempt to penetrate to those within. The excited curiosity and tireless ingenuity of an age, emancipated from a hundred inhibitions, penetrates into every secret corner of the mind, and, without effort, floats out on its spate of waters, creations of the mind which the individual, in whom they lay hidden, once brought slowly and painfully to the light of day. Too well practiced in insight to pause, this age suddenly finds itself at landlocked waters, where, perhaps, no age has ever yet been without divine pretext, and in full publicity; exploring everywhere, it turns workshops into exhibition grounds and has no objection to taking its meals among the stores. It may be right, for it derives from the future. It occupies our minds in a manner in which no age has, for a long time, occupied those inhabiting it; it pushes and displaces and makes a clearance, each of us has much for which to thank it. And yet who has not watched it, at least for a moment, with mistrust; and asked himself if it is really concerned with fruitfulness, or only with a mechanically better and more exhaustive exploitation of the soul? It confuses us with ever new possibilities of perception; but how much has it put before us which has caused no corresponding progress in our inner life? Now, I will, to be sure, assume that it offered, at the same time, to our determined youth the most unexpected means of gradually giving outward, visible form in precise equivalents to their purest inner realities; indeed, I am prepared to believe it possesses these means in the highest degree. But, while I hold myself ready to attribute to it, our age, various new artistic gains, my admiration passes on and beyond to the poems, which remain always, now no less than before, incomprehensible.

Even if there were not one among the younger poets who did not rejoice to profit in his outlook by the daring and intensified spirit of our time, I should, indeed, not be afraid of having treated too seriously the question of the poetic essence and its establishment in the life within. All simplifications, however penetrating, do not take effect in that region where the difficult rejoices that it is difficult. After all, what can alter the situation of one who, from his early days, has been destined to set in motion supreme forces within his own heart, forces which others hold at bay in theirs and reduce to silence? And what kind of peace could be imagined for him when, within, he is suffering the assault of his god?

Primal Sound

RAINER MARIA RILKE

At the time when I was in school, the phonograph must just have been invented. Anyhow, public wonder about it was at its highest pitch, and thus it may be explained that our physics teacher, a man always inclined to busy himself with mechanical toys, instructed us how to put together, out of the most easily accessible materials, a similar apparatus. No more was needed than what I shall here set forth: a piece of flexible cardboard, folded into a funnel whose narrower, round opening was then sealed with a piece of impermeable paper such as is used to seal glasses of preserves, thereby improvising a vibrating membrane, in whose middle we next stuck a bristle from a stout clothes-brush, extending vertically. With these few materials the one part of the mysterious machine was set up; both receiver and transmitter were entirely ready, and there now remained but to devise a cylinder, which, turned by a small crank, could be pushed close against the cutting pin. I do not recall from what we made it. Some sort of cylinder we discovered, and with indifferent success coated it with a thin layer of candle wax. Scarcely was it cold and hard before we shoved one another aside to put our work to the test, our impatience having been heightened by all this pasting and doing. Nothing more is needed to imagine what happened. If someone spoke or sang into the horn, the pin stuck in the parchment transferred the sound waves on to the impressionable surface as it rolled slowly past, and if the zealous pointer were permitted at once to retrace its own path (fixed in the mean-

"Ur-Geräusch" was first published in *Das Inselschiff* (Leipzig), I (1919), 14-20, and is reprinted in Rilke's *Gesammelte Werke*, Insel-Verlag, Leipzig, 1927, Bd. IV, pp. 285-294. Translated by Carl Niemeyer in Rainer Maria Rilke, *Primal Sound and Other Prose Pieces*, Cummington Press, Cummington, Mass., 1947, pp. 33-38. Revised by the editors.

time by a varnish), there trembled and faltered back to us from the paper funnel the sound which had just been our own, uncertain, to be sure, indescribably faint and timid and in places failing altogether. The effect was always most overwhelming. Our class was not of the quietest, and not many times before could it have been capable of attaining a similar degree of common silence. The amazing, even unnerving impact of the phenomenon lost nothing by repetition. We stood, as it were, in the presence of a new, infinitely tender particle of reality, out of which there spoke to us, children though we were, something far beyond our comprehension, yet so ineffably tentative, in such need of help that our hearts were touched. Then and in the years to come, I thought, this independent sound, abstracted from us and preserved outside us, would never be forgotten. That it came about otherwise is the cause of this account. As I shall show, not the sound from the horn remained dominant in my mind, but much more particularly those marks cut into the cylinder.

Since that time in school fourteen or fifteen years may have passed, when one day this came into my consciousness. It was while I was first in Paris and attending with considerable enthusiasm the anatomy lectures at the École des Beaux Arts. My interest, it seemed, lay not so much in the manifold network of muscles and sinews or in the mutual understanding of the inner organs, but rather in the arid skeleton, whose repressed energy and elasticity I had already glimpsed in the pages of Leonardo. Much, however, as I now puzzled over the structural whole, it was too much for me. My attention always focused itself upon an exploration of the skull, in which this chalky element seemed to me to have attained its uttermost, as though precisely here it had been persuaded to exert itself meaningfully to a definite function—so that it might take under firm protection something ultimately dangerous, something, though narrowly enclosed, yet boundlessly active. The enchantment I found in this peculiar container, shutting out the vastness of the whole world, was at length so great that I procured myself a skull in order to spend with it many an hour of the night. And, as always happens to me with things, it was not only the moments of purposeful study that remarkably assimilated this ambiguous object to me. My intimacy with it I owe no doubt in some degree to those roving glances with which we involuntarily probe and comprehend our customary surroundings, if they but have some relation to us. Such a glance I suddenly stopped in its course and fixed clearly and attentively. In the often so peculiarly living and challenging light of the candle the coronal suture had just become sharply visible, and I knew immediately too of what it reminded me—of one of those unforgotten furrows such as the point of a bristle had cut into a little roll of wax!

And now I do not know: is it not a rhythmic peculiarity of my imagination that since then, often at long intervals of years, the impulse ever again arises in me to leap from this instantly perceived similarity to a whole series of fabulous experiments? I confess at once that I have treated the desire, as often as it appeared, never otherwise than with the greatest mistrust. Were proof of this needed, it would lie in the circumstance that I only now, again more than a decade and a half later, have decided upon a cautious communication. Nor can I adduce in favor of my fancy any more than its persistent return, through which, without any connection with my other affairs, it has in first one place then another surprised me under the most various circumstances.

What is it then that persists in suggesting itself? It is this:

The coronal suture of the skull (which should now be chiefly investigated) has—let us assume—a certain similarity to the closely wound line that the needle of a phonograph cuts into the receptive, revolving cylinder of the machine. Suppose, for instance, one played a trick on this needle and caused it to retrace a path not made by the graphic translation of a sound, but self-sufficing and existing in nature—well, let us say it boldly, even along the coronal suture—what would happen? A sound must come into being, a sequence of sounds, music. . . .

Feelings—of what sort? Incredulity, awe, fear, reverence—yes, which of all of these feelings prevents me from proposing a name for the primal sound that would then come to birth? . . .

Assume for a moment: could one not foist upon the needle

lines from anywhere and put them to the test? What contour could one not thus draw out in order to perceive it, transformed, making its impact upon another sense?

At a certain time when I was beginning to concern myself with Arabian poetry, in whose origin the five senses seem to have a more simultaneous and more equivalent share, it first struck me how dissimilar and sporadic is the contemporary European poet's use of these talebearers, only one of which—sight—overcharged with perception, continually engulfs him. How small in contrast is the contribution of the inattentive hearing, to say nothing of the indifference of the remaining senses, which, functioning discontinuously and apart, exert themselves only in their own conveniently confined territories. And yet the finished poem can come about only on condition that the world, simultaneously grasped by these five levers, appear under a given aspect upon that supernatural plane which is precisely the plane of poetry.

A woman to whom such was proposed in a conversation exclaimed that this wonderful capability and achievement of all the senses acting at the same time is nothing else but presence of the spirit and grace of love—and in saying this she gave good testimony besides to the sublime reality of poetry. But for this very reason the lover is in tremendous danger, because he is thrown into the midst of the interplay of his senses, which he knows are only by accident in that peculiar, dangerous medium where, losing all breadth, they converge and where nothing lasts.

While I so express myself, I have before me the sketch I used as a welcome aid whenever similar considerations intruded upon me. If one pictures to himself in a completed circle the whole range of the world's experience as well as the regions beyond us, it becomes instantly clear how much greater are the black sectors, which indicate what we may not experience, as compared to the irregular light sections, which correspond to the searchlights of sensuality.

Now the situation of the lover is this, that he feels himself set unawares in the middle of the circle at a point where the known and the incomprehensible rush to converge, become complete, and become pure possession, to be sure, with the total loss of detail. This displacement would be no service to the poet. For him the manifold details must remain present; he is obligated to use the regions of the senses to their fullest extent, and hence he must also desire to extend each separate one as far as possible, so that the leap of his interwoven rapture through the five gardens may succeed in one single breath.

If the danger of the lover consists in his restricted viewpoint, that of the poet is his awareness of the abysses which divide one order of perception from the others: in fact, they are of such vastness and suction as to be able to wrest the greater part of the world—and who knows of how many worlds?—past us and away from us.

The question arises here whether the work of the scientist may essentially broaden the extent of these sectors on the plane we have pictured. Rather, will not the gains of the microscope, the telescope, and the many contrivances that introduce the senses into new regions either below or above, finally rest upon another level, since the greatest increase so gained cannot be penetrated by the senses and hence not really "experienced"? It is not rash to suppose that the artist, in developing this (if it may be so called) five-fingered hand of his senses to an ever more active and more spiritual grasp, works most definitely toward an extension of the regions of the individual senses. Unfortunately, the proof of his accomplishment, which is ultimately impossible without the marvelous, does not allow him to put upon the unfolded, common map the regions personally conquered.

However, to one searching for a means to bring about the finally crucial union of areas so strangely sundered, what could be more promising than the very experiment recommended in the first pages of this reminiscence? If it is again proposed here at the end, with the reservation mentioned previously, may the writer be given credit for resisting the temptation to enlarge arbitrarily upon assumptions conceived in the free play of his fancy. The assignment, passed over for so many years and constantly reappearing, seemed to him too limited and too explicit.

Concerning La Symphonie pastorale

ANDRÉ GIDE

I am sure there is not one of my books whose subject I carried longer in my head—Paul-Albert Laurens remembers that I talked to him about it during our trip to Biskra in 1893. And yet, it is the one book which I would most readily give up, if I knew that in exchange for this sacrifice, I could make the others immortal.

The praises which it receives these days from certain critics do not seem so much exaggerated as out of balance with the slight attention given to others of my books which I consider more important, such as *Les Caves du Vatican*. And it seems to me that even among my short narratives, this one is less opportune than *L'Immoraliste*, less pathetic than *La Porte étroite*, and less successful than *Isabelle*. But success rarely coincides with merit, and it may well be that certain critics felt they had not quite caught up with me.

Some friends who, I hope, were not wrong in expecting a richer and more individual work from me, have asked me why I wasted my ink and my energy on a subject which no longer interested me and on a form which did not interest me at all. Shall I reply that it is my nature always to put off what is best? I would be glad to write at the end of each of my books: "What is most important remains to be said." First of all, I took care to make sure that someone was interested. Also, I was moving out of a long period of intellectual inactivity, full of doubts, apprehensions, modesty; I wanted to exercise my pen once more, and to try it again on a subject of not too great importance, as I had earlier done with *Le Retour de l'enfant prodigue*, following another period of inhibition. . . . But particularly this subject dis-

"A propos de la *Symphonie pastorale*" was first published in *Hommage à André Gide*, La Nouvelle Revue Française, Paris, 1951, pp. 377-379, from a manuscript belonging to the Bibliothèque Littéraire Jacques Doucet of the University of Paris. Translated by Haskell M. Block.

turbed me, imposed itself, and I felt that I could not attach myself to anything else with a free spirit before I had finished it off.
It was the last of the projects of my youth, beyond which I saw
nothing else that would keep me from finally working freely—
I mean, without a preconceived plan. For up to this time I did
nothing but bring older plans to completion. Not one of my
books was not conceived and virtually completely designed between the ages of twenty and thirty, or, to be more exact, between twenty and twenty-five. For each of them it was like a
sudden illumination, the book appearing to me all at once, like
an unfamiliar landscape at the sudden flash of lightning on a
stormy night. (Léon Daudet has said something similar about his
father's books, if I remember correctly, and I am not sure that
I have not borrowed his image. It could not be put more exactly.
Yes, everything appears to you all at once, down to the smallest
detail, but so fleetingly that you must afterwards make a patient
effort to restore and reconstitute what you were not able earlier
to make out clearly enough.) From the age of twenty-five, my
books were there, set out before me; I had only to write them.
I have taken the time to do so.

All this doubtlessly explains the weakness of most of them:
the constriction of their last parts, so hurried am I to have done
with them and to go on to something else. It also explains this
state of anachronism I always feel in relation to my writing[1]—a
condition which, on the other hand, permits the freest play of
critical intelligence, and that domination of the subject which
M. Benda admires so much when he meets it in others besides
myself, but it retains the fertility and the sort of immediate, irresponsible, and frequently almost unconscious flux for which I
would give all the qualities vaunted by M. Benda.

This is also why, for a long time, I have not allowed myself
to carry new projects inside me or, at least, to plan out anything
in advance.

---

1. In order to carry *La Symphonie pastorale* to a proper conclusion,
I had to torture myself; for nothing was more different from what I
deliberately wanted to write than these subtleties, these nuances, which
my subject forced upon me. Nothing has disgusted me more.

Paul Valéry

ANDRÉ GIDE

Nothing could do greater honor to our Provisional Government than the magnificent funeral officially bestowed on Paul Valéry, with a pomp and circumstance worthy of that most eminent representative of the genius of France—Paul Valéry, thanks to whose shining light our country still keeps her supreme rank in the spiritual world, in spite of our historic reverses and our apparent wretchedness. Such recognition is as astonishing as it is remarkable, for Paul Valéry's outstanding value is of the kind that does not appeal to popular favor. That it was indirectly and, as it were, unintentionally, of immense service to France is a fact that could be appreciated only by very few. His activity was unconcerned with public affairs and was exercised in a region set apart, aloof from events, but one where, unknown to ourselves, our destinies are being played for. "Events bore me," he used to say. "Events are the froth of circumstance. It's the sea I'm interested in. It's the sea we fish in; the sea we sail on; the sea we dive into."

And no one ever dived deeper than he.

From his early youth he was stirred by a secret ambition. I cannot imagine a nobler one. Compared with it, that of Balzac's heroes only raises a smile. But even on the profane and worldly plane that is theirs, Valéry succeeded as well as, and indeed better, than any of them. He knew how honors are won; he knew what they are worth and what they cost in peace of mind. He was will-

First published in *L'Arche*, No. 10, October, 1945, pp. 3-17, and reprinted in *New Writing and Daylight*, VII, John Lehmann, London, 1946, pp. 98-108. Translated by Dorothy Bussy.

ing to pay the price, if only to show others and prove to himself that there was nothing in them out of his reach. What he wanted was the right to despise such things. For his inclination was to despise things in general. There lies his strength. The domination he desired was of a different kind—the domination of the mind itself. Anything else seemed to him derisory. To dominate not the minds of others, but his own; to know its working, to make himself master of that, in order to use it as he chose. It was toward this that his efforts were constantly directed. A queer kind of Narcissus, wishing to dominate Mind by means of Mind. Anything more than that was of no interest to him; not the object itself, no; but the means of obtaining it—when he wished —how he wished; *to be able* to. . . . "My nature," he would say, "is potential." It is fortunate for us that Valéry chose to apply his method to literary ends. "The field of letters," said he, "is the one in which I thought it would be easiest to exist." From hence-forward, he considered his most admirable poems, his most ac-complished prose in the light of *exercises*[1]—"Q.E.D.'s." This is how he spoke of his *Jeune Parque.* And I have no doubt that he could have exercised the sovereign method he applied here in any other field and with the same triumphant results. Yes; I can easily imagine Paul Valéry a great statesman, a great diplomat, a finan-cier, a man of science, an engineer, or a doctor. And I even won-der whether he might not have been as eminent in architecture, painting, or music as he was in poetry; though these, indeed, re-quire special gifts. But Valéry possessed those gifts, too, in almost equal measure.

Like Edgar Allan Poe, he started from this principle—that the artist, be he painter, poet, or musician, must take as the ground on which to build, not his own emotion but that which he wishes to excite in his listener, his spectator, or his reader. Like the actor Diderot holds up to our admiration in his *Paradoxe sur le Com-édien*, his business is not to be moved but to move. This was Leonardo da Vinci's and Wagner's procedure. Valéry would not believe in the Romantics' "Muse," and made a mock of what is

---

1. "Everything I think about art is related to the idea of *exercise.*"

called "Inspiration." He would willingly have taken as his motto Flaubert's saying, "Inspiration? It consists in sitting down to one's writing table every day at the same time." To the very end of his life, Valéry rose before dawn and, till other people disturbed him by waking, he worked.

He worked, I suppose, in the same way as Descartes, not precisely at any special task, but at pursuing his thoughts to their last entrenchments. During nearly twenty years, while his companions of early days were striving over productions which he considered of slight importance, Valéry was silently searching. When confronted with any work of value, he would ask himself, "How was it done?" The made dish appealed to him far less than the recipe. He scorned chance flashes of genius. And in particular, he couldn't endure being taken in. When we were still quite young (we were barely twenty when there began between us that inestimable intercourse which was only to end with his death) he pinned up on his bedroom wall the famous maxim (I have forgotten the Greek), "Never cease to mistrust." And, in fact, he treated everything with mistrust—human beings, objects, convictions, professions of faith, faith itself; and above all, words—and we know what latent energy is released by the disintegration of those dangerous atoms.

I remember one evening his reading aloud to me one or another of Maurice Barrès' eloquent speeches (we were sitting together in a little café in the Boulevard St. Germain, near the Ministry of War, where, at that time Valéry filled some very insignificant post). With a smile, he raised his voice oratorically, then, diverging from the text, but without changing his tone and as though continuing to read from it, he finally wound up, "And we see rising before us the specter of (here a pause) *hideous* facility!" The scorn and horror he felt for all facility lay at the bottom of those inflexible demands he made upon himself—demands which were to carry him so far. In the meantime he *produced nothing*.

His silence began at last to make us uneasy; some of us would speak of it ironically. "And what about your great Valéry, who made such a brilliant start? He was stopped short at those few early poems of his. Full of promise, no doubt, but now he's turned silent. He'll always be silent. You must admit you rather over-rated him. He has petered out already. . . ." He began to be taken for a "would be" and already almost for a "might-have-been."

His talk, however, was as dazzling as ever. So much so that I began to fear that he would rest satisfied with that. I was anxious too lest, with his love of precision, the attraction of mathematics might prove too much for him. In those days it was not at a table that he worked, with a sheet or two of white paper, but at an enormous blackboard, which was very much in the way in the humble little room he lived in at that time.[2] He used to draw strange signs on it, complicated equations, and I understood not a word of the formulas, which he insisted on explaining to me lengthily, in spite of my incompetence; for he cared very little whether he was understood or not, and it was more for himself or to himself that he talked, than to others. This was the reason too, that he paid so little attention to his enunciation which all his life was exceedingly indistinct. It often happened that the flocks of faithful that sat under him at the Collège de France, the Vieux Colombier, the Sorbonne, or elsewhere, had to be content with seeing him and give up any hope of understanding him, unable as they were to ask him to repeat his words, as was possible in private conversation. For that matter, he was often satisfied with any listener who seemed sufficiently attentive and allowed him to flow on to his heart's content, without interrupting him. In the days of our youth, he used to sing the praises of a certain "inter-locutor," who was as deferential and silent as could be wished, drinking in his words and content with expressing his rapt admiration by looks alone. Valéry used to meet him every day at the same hour on the outside of a bus. This unknown individual aroused my curiosity. I was jealous of him. Who could he be? . . . After a series of investigations, I discovered at last that he was the swimming master of the Rochechouart swimming baths.

It was mathematics that chiefly occupied his thoughts at this time, not at first geometry, for which he began by showing an utter lack of comprehension. "When," he said, "at school, I first

---

2. Impasse Royer-Collard at the end of the Rue Gay-Lussac.

heard a professor say, 'Take the triangle *ABC* and superimpose it on the triangle *ABC*,' my brain refused to follow.[3] What on earth could it mean? It's useless to go on. I'll have none of it." Let others judge if such an exclusion of geometry is reasonable. I doubt whether Valéry was able to keep it up, seeing that, on the other hand, he went on undauntedly with the study of astronomy. He gave Lobatchevsky, Clerk Maxwell, and Riemann an attention he denied all purely literary works. Once, when he was staying with me at La Roque, he was delighted to find on his bedside table a copy of Clerk Maxwell's works which I had had the pleasure of getting for him. One evening he took down from my shelves the two volumes of Dickens' *Martin Chuzzlewit*, which he returned next morning, saying he had spent part of the night reading them.

"What!" I cried, "all through?"

"Oh! Quite enough. I'm acquainted now with the book's general run, which is pleasing enough. I've seen where it starts from and where it gets to. Between the two, it's just filling up. A good secretary who had caught the hang of it, would have done very nearly as well. The *farà da sé* doesn't interest me."

He was very quick to assimilate the small amount of nourishment to be found in a book, and oftener than not, once he had gathered the gist of it, his curiosity passed on to other things. Lingering, even among delights, gave him no pleasure. *Ars non stagnat* was his motto; and, as he esteemed a work of art only so far as the artist could reproduce it at will, "Why reproduce," thought he, "what has already been done to perfection?" The important thing was to bring each undertaking to perfection as quickly as possible, so as to be able to leave it then and there. And so, after he had got his hand in by the "exercises" of the *Jeune Parque*, he went on to perfect, one after the other, those accomplished works, his great poems. He went forward unceasingly, thinking it a shame to hide his gropings, his retouches, his

---

3. He recurred to this incidentally in 1934 when in his essay, *Fluctuations sur la Liberté*, he wrote, "I cannot even conceive the equality of figures as used in geometry."

first drafts, leaving his fellow writers behind to go on inde-
fatigably repeating the same verses, the same books, or, without
having made any progress, their equivalents.

He had, in fact, no little contempt for literature, and particularly for novels. The truth is, he was not interested in other people, at any rate as individuals, for he refused to give in to—I was
going to say—sympathy, but I don't want the word to be misunderstood, or that it should be thought I mean he was incapable
of affection. No; only that he was unwilling to allow the thoughts
or emotions of others to trespass, by contagion, on his own
domain. Wasn't this what La Rochefoucauld meant when he
wrote, "I am little susceptible to pity and wish I were not so at
all"?

In consequence, his admirations in the field of letters were
rare, more and more grudging, and quickly outgrown or outworn. I was astonished to find, for instance, that the feeling he
had at first professed for Stendhal[4] made him smile at the latter
end of his life; he then paradoxically declared that he preferred
Restif de la Bretonne or Casanova. For that matter he read little,
feeling no need to have recourse to others in order himself to
think.

I believe, however, that his devotion to Mallarmé persisted unaltered. He looked on him as his master and predecessor in the
arduous path he himself was to tread after him, but in which, as
I think, he was soon to surpass him. With all this, Valéry was one
of the most faithful of friends. "I am in love with friendship,"
he might have said with Montesquieu. Notwithstanding his aversion to sentimentality, he gave his intimates many proofs of the
sensibility and tenderness of his heart, but also of his extreme
reserve, which was so great that he would, no doubt, blame me
for mentioning them. This reputed cynic was capable of the most
exquisite attention and kindnesses toward the people he was attached to. Now that he is no longer with us, I may be permitted
to tell how, shortly after Mallarmé's death, he came to me saying,

---

4. "I have no interest in, I have no need of his emotions," he said of
Stendhal in particular. "I only want him to instruct me as to his methods."

"There is some talk of putting up a memorial to him and there will be, very properly, lists of subscribers in the newspapers. But Mallarmé has left a widow and daughter in the apartment we used to go to so often, and its rent has to be paid. How? Nobody cares about that. I'm not able to undertake this expense by myself, but I thought you might perhaps help me. You won't say anything about it though, will you?"

Throughout his life he was preoccupied by money matters and was in constant fear of running short. It was this, as well as his desire to oblige, that prevented him disentangling himself from the unending demands, solicitations, requests to which he was subject. Hence, his innumerable addresses and prefaces. "People," he wrote, "seem not to understand or not to believe—and yet I have repeated it often enough—that the greater part of my work has been written in *answer* to requests or to chance circumstances, and that without these solicitations or necessities coming from outside, it would not exist." The excessive number of engagements with which he allowed himself to be burdened, exhausted him. He longed to throw up the sponge and beg for mercy. "All these overcharming persons," he said, "will kill me. Do you know the epitaph that ought to be inscribed on my tomb? Here lies Paul Valéry, done to death by others." Nevertheless, it must be acknowledged that many of his best pages were elicited in this way. For that matter, nothing he wrote could afford to be neglected. Dipping into his accumulated reserves, he scattered his treasures about him in a sparkling shower. His writings, however, were of so rare a quality that they appealed only to a restricted public. His books were not best sellers. Their teaching could be understood only by an élite, and indeed, it was not desirable it should reach a larger circle, for like Nietzsche's, it might very well lead astray those readers it fails to invigorate.

His reputation, meanwhile, soon spread, and not only in France. Cecil Rhodes, having heard Valéry well spoken of, I don't exactly know by whom, sent for him to London when he was still quite young, to entrust him with some highly important work. Bound over to secrecy and moreover little given to being expansive, it was to very few people that Valéry confided this extraordinary adventure, which was particularly surprising in such an uneventful life as his. As soon as he got back from London, where his mysterious task kept him some weeks, he told me the story, which I barely remember, of the strange conditions to which he had been subjected. As for the nature of the work itself, his vow of silence forbade him to say a single word concerning it. I only heard that immediately on arrival in England, he was met by an individual whose name he never learned, and then taken to London and deposited in a kind of apartment which was comfortable but hermetically sealed from the outer world. During the whole of his stay he was not once allowed out and was forbidden to communicate with a living soul. A servant who was either a real or pretense deaf-mute or someone who knew no common language, brought him his meals every day and went away again without having opened his lips. This almost pleasant jail ended only when Valéry had finished his job. He was then taken back to the port where he had landed, by the same individual who had met him, and kept only a dreamlike memory of the whole affair.

Certain journalists have mentioned a situation he is said to have taken at the Agence Havas in 1900 and kept for a considerable time. This is not quite the case. The truth is that old M. Lebey, the founder of the famous Agency, engaged him as his private secretary, reader, and adviser—a confidential post, in which Valéry had ample opportunities of exercising his sagacity, his competence in political, diplomatic, and financial matters, the sureness of his judgment, his probity, his tact, and finally, the exquisite courtesy of his manners and the sensitiveness of his feelings. He used to speak of the old gentleman, to whom he became much attached, with great deference; "something like old M. Leuwen," he would say. He suffered from a form of trembling paralysis which deprived him of the control of his movements. When people came to see him, as he was unable to hold out his hand because of its shaking, he would say, "Please hold on to my hand." Seated in a big armchair, he used to listen to Valéry reading aloud the newspapers or Bourdaloue's sermons, which he preferred to Bossuet's; but Valéry confessed to me that he used often to skip whole pages. This lasted months and years. He no doubt learned a great deal in the company of this wise old man and in the discharge of his delicate duties, which brought into play the practical qualities of his mind. When, leaving the abstract region of mathematics, he turned his eyes on the present day world (*Regards sur le Monde Actuel*), his views and judgments were so far-seeing that they strike us now as being prophetic, and I think that at that time no one can have had a sounder appreciation of the situation in Europe and France.

What he wrote in 1927 on the subject of the French nation is still strikingly applicable and remarkably appropriate at the present time:

"This country, full of nerves and contrasts as she is, finds unexpected resources in those very contrasts. The secret of her prodigious power of resistance lies, perhaps, in the great and manifold differences that she combines within herself. In the French people, apparent lightness of character is accompanied by singular endurance and resilience. The general ease and pleasantness of social relations in France are accompanied by a critical acuteness which is always on the alert. Perhaps she is the only country in which ridicule has played a historic part; governments have been undermined and overthrown by it, and a witticism or a happy—sometimes too happy—thrust is enough, in the eyes of the public, to damage, almost instantaneously, powers and reputations of the highest importance. *On the other hand, a kind of natural indiscipline may be observed among the French, which always gives way when the necessity for discipline becomes evident. It happens that the nation is suddenly found to be united at the very moment that it might have been expected to be divided.*"

Before retreating into silence, Valéry consented to publish two works, one immediately after the other, in two different reviews—"La Méthode de Léonard de Vinci" (1894) in Madame Adam's *Nouvelle Revue* and, in *Le Centaure*, at that time edited by Pierre Louys, the astounding "Soirée avec M. Teste" (1895). To that extraordinary creation, unparalleled in any other tongue, to that accomplished and perfect work, each one of us was compelled to do homage. As he had just disclosed his method to us through the medium of Leonardo, Valéry, thanks to this semi-mythical alibi, here revealed his ethic, his attitude towards things, beings, ideas, life. This he maintained and to the end remained faithful—constant to himself, so that a little while before his death he was able to say (I quote his very words), "The principal themes around which for fifty years I have grouped my thoughts are still in my mind UNSHAKABLE." He spoke this last word strongly, accentuating each syllable.

But let there be no mistake. Monsieur Teste is not Valéry, but only a projection of him—of a Valéry stripped of the playfulness, the poetic humor, the charming grace, of everything, in fact, that made us love him. Doubtless he considered all the stir and bustle that went on around him as vanity and worthy only of a passing attention, but more often, as long as he was not disturbed by it, he looked on it with indulgence or even with the kind of amusement we sometimes take in the trifling games of children. I remember in bygone days with what amazing gusto he manipulated the marionettes of a little Punch and Judy theatre, in order to entertain his family circle, just as, at a later time, he lent himself to the play of society conversation and drawing-room comedy. For that matter he enjoyed it; petted, made much of, listening very little, talking a great deal, sparkling with wit, he was manifestly amused by his easy successes, or rather, by the very ease with which he won his successes. Even with his intimates, the gravity of his thoughts never clouded the amenity of his temper. Nothing can be more instructive on this point than Madame Teste's fictitious letter—an incomparable work of exquisite delicacy and a singular revelation of our mathematician's secret sensibility. "I think," he makes Madame Teste say, rather plaintively, of her terrible husband, "I think he is too logical in his ideas." And in another passage (*Orientem Versus*) Valéry, fully conscious of the deadly danger of being too implacably rigorous, writes, "I'm impatient of vagueness. It's a kind of malady—a peculiar irritability, directed against life, for life would be impossible if we refused to accept the *near enough*."

Yes, literature is laid over a ground of *near enough*; it's in the *near enough* that we are all floundering. I was only too much aware of this in his presence, and the charm of his manner did not always prevent me from feeling abashed. It was his great respect for others, as well as his own indifference, that enabled him to tolerate a religious turn of mind, but solely in others, for, needless to say, he himself refused to accept any creed whatever. He had a particular aversion to Protestantism, which strips the Christian religion of all that Catholicism has bestowed on it—of outward charm, of political order in its structure, of practical application in its relationships. So that he took sides with the Jesuits and against Pascal. He had, moreover, a loathing of religious phraseology and, indeed, for all vague expressions. To such *assignats,* paper money with nothing behind them, he would give no credit. And this reminds me of an absurd example of that delightful vivacity of which I was speaking just now:

A slight feverish attack had kept me in bed for several days. He came to see me and as he sat by my bedside, we had a long talk. What about? The Christian virtues, I believe. And as I took up their defense, I let fall the word "abnegation." Paul started up, sprang from his chair and rushed to the door in feigned agitation:

"Ice!" he shouted. "Quick! Bring some ice! The patient is delirious! He is abnegating!" —thus inventing an impossible French word—"Il abnègue."

Full of deference for others, I said, but not of reverence. Deference is a first convenient stage on the road to veneration, and veneration implies respect. Now Valéry knew how much respect interferes with us. "The white man possesses a quality which has enabled him to make his way—disrespect," writes Henri Michaux, disrespectfully. Valéry, whose mind wanted "to make its way," was not to be stopped by any form of laziness. He said laughingly (or did he write it?), "It's curious how many people lose their lives in accidents for want of letting go their umbrellas!" To get rid of all impediments was his constant preoccupation, and it is impossible to imagine a freer mind than his.

Don't let people accuse me, as they have so often done in the cases of Dostoievsky, Goethe, and Montaigne, of putting my own color on Valéry. Nothing could be more different than our two natures, nothing more contrary than the bent of our two minds. Mine "naturally inclined to veneration," as Goethe said of his own, as much as Valéry's was resolutely bent on impiety, antagonistic to all accepted and unverified beliefs, resolutely skeptical (at once doubting and seeking), regardless of agreement, approval, or sympathy and apparently free from all human weaknesses, vain curiosities, adventitious preoccupations, procrastinations, sentimental dallyings. To everything likely to distract him from his quest, he said "NO!" Whereas I, if like him and in his wake I had doubts, it was, above all, of myself. He seemed barely aware of his ascendancy. My friendship submitted to it, not without some kicking, but the small resistance I attempted to offer him rapidly broke down and retreated in discomfiture. But one thing was clear to me, of which I never doubted—that he was always right. His scorn occasionally hurt me, at least at some points, but I acknowledged he had the right to be scornful—a right he had won in hard-fought battle. His stark, iconoclastic hammer spared nothing. And in those days I was incapable of answering his quips ironically, as I did a short time before the war at a meeting of the Radio Committee, when I had the pleasure of sitting beside him at the green table. *A propos* of some broadcast, the name of Homer came up, and Valéry bent toward me and whispered, "Have you ever read anything more boring than the *Iliad?*" "Yes," I answered, "the *Chanson de Roland.*" (If I had been a little more on the spot I should have said, *La Jeune Parque.*)

Not that, as time went on, I took him less seriously (I am almost tempted to say, "On the contrary"), but I, on my part, had become more sure of myself. In the first days to which my memories of Paul Valéry go back, I would generally come away from our talks with a shaken mind and heart. "He breaks your spirit with a single word," writes Madame Teste of her husband, "and I feel like a spoiled pot, thrown away by the potter on to his heap of failures." Yes; that was the very thing I felt too. And she adds, "He is hard as an angel"; and again, "His existence seems to put in doubt everybody else's." My admiration must have been lively indeed for my friendship not to have been too severely wounded. Nothing that I lived for seemed to have any value in his eyes, and I could not believe that he had the smallest consideration for anything I had written or wished to write. To have thought this due to any insufficiency on his part would have seemed to me presumption on mine. But he managed to show me his affection in so discreet—so almost tender a fashion—that it went to my heart more surely than any effusions. Nothing could have flattered, nothing could have touched me more, than his reliance on my literary taste, when he called me in for consultation on some poem he had just elaborated; nothing could have shown me better that he attached importance, at any rate, to my judgment. Doubtless confidences were distasteful to him, and as he considered confessions a shocking form of exhibitionism, he disliked what I liked and what I considered it my duty to write, but he esteemed that I knew how to write and that esteem was enough for me.[5]

I was greatly surprised one day by the unexpected praise he gave me for an article of mine to which, I confess, I attached very little importance; it was the *Dialogue with a German*, written shortly after the other war.

"But it's mere reporting," I protested.

"No matter!" he went on. "Its line is perfect."

I believe this was the only praise he ever gave me, at any rate, as far as I can remember.

May the portrait I have tried to trace of him here be one that would have pleased him!

Admirable as most of Valéry's poems seem to us, I am not sure that I do not prefer his prose; many of his pages, I believe, will remain among the most perfect that have ever been written in any language. Let me add at once that I know few French writers,

---

5. I am not speaking here of the Valéry of early days, but of what he became later, of what he made himself become.

if indeed I know any (in Germany there is Goethe), who have excelled equally in both forms. And without any doubt, it is from his prose that I expect the most salutary, the most efficacious action. For it concerns me very little that a certain number of writers modified their theory and practice of poetry to follow in his footsteps, and that a quantity of apprentice hands were induced to versify in imitation of him. This turn of the helm against the current of excessive license well deserved to be given, but it is on quite another plane and in a more veiled manner that the extraordinary benefit of Valéry's influence was exercised. This *asper contemptor deum* seems to me, above all, a master liberator. No one—not even Voltaire himself—ever did more to emancipate us, to wean us from faiths, cults, beliefs. At the very moment that France, bleeding from her wounds, seems ready to fly for refuge to religious devotion and seek there consolation and salvation (as she did at the end of Louis XIV's reign, after our military reverses, when the bigotry of the age, in conjunction with his own, drove Racine to silence), Valéry's virile teaching takes on special importance, as did the example of his resistance compared with the base compliance of others. "NO" he said obstinately, and stood, a living testimony of the unbowed and unconquerable mind.

"But how comes it," he would say to me, "that men take their rest so soon? Why are they content with so little?"

A la Recherche du Temps Perdu

MARCEL PROUST

I am now publishing but one volume, *Du côté de chez Swann*, of a novel that will have for its complete title *A la Recherche du Temps Perdu*. I should have preferred publishing it all at once, but works in several volumes are no longer published. I am like a person who has a tapestry too large for the walls of his rooms and who has had to cut it.

On the contrary, the young writers today, with whom I sympathize in all other matters, lavish their praise on novels of compact action and few characters. This is not my conception of the novel. Do you want to know what I mean? You know that there is a plane geometry and a geometry in space. Well, then, for me, the novel belongs not only to plane psychology but to psychology in time. I have tried to isolate this invisible substance of time, but this required that the attempt be a sustained and durable one. I hope that at the end of my book, an incidental and unimportant social event, such as the marriage of two persons who, in the first volume, belong to completely different worlds, will indicate that time has passed and will take on that beauty of certain patina-covered lead roofs of Versailles, which time has encased in a sheath of emerald.

Then, like a city that we see from a train following its contorted route, now on our right side, now on our left, the various appearances that a single character will have had in the eyes of another—to the point that he must have been like a series of different characters—will convey, by this means only, the sensation of past time. Such characters will reveal themselves later on as

This essay is taken from remarks made by Marcel Proust in an interview published under the above title in *Le Temps* (Paris), November 13, 1913. Translated by Haskell M. Block.

different from what they are in the first volume, different from what might be expected, as happens, indeed, very often in life.

There are not only the same characters reappearing in the course of this work in various roles, as in some of Balzac's cycles, but there are in a single character certain deep, almost unconscious impressions.

From this point of view, my book might perhaps be something like an attempt at a series of "Novels of the Unconscious." I should not be ashamed to say "Bergson novels" if I believed this were so, for in any age literature tries to attach itself, after the fact, of course, to the dominant philosophy of the time. But this would not be accurate, for my work is dominated by the distinction between the involuntary memory and the voluntary memory, a distinction which not only does not occur in Bergson's philosophy, but is even contradicted by it.

For me, the voluntary memory, which is especially a memory exercised by intelligence and sight, gives us only false shadows of the past; but an odor or a scent recurring in completely different circumstances awakens the past in us in spite of ourselves, and we realize how different this past was from what we imagined we recalled, and that our voluntary memory painted like bad painters, with colors that have no truth. Already in this first volume, you will see the character who narrates, who says "I" (and who is not me), suddenly find again forgotten years, gardens, persons, in the taste of a sip of tea in which he found a piece of little cake called a *madeleine*: of course he remembered them, but without their color, without their charm; I have made him say that just as in that little Japanese game in which you wet loosely folded pieces of paper that, as soon as they are dropped into a bowl, expand, twist and turn, and become flowers or people, so all the flowers of his garden, and the water lilies of the Vivonne, and the good people of the village and their little homes and the church, and all Combray and its surroundings, all taking form and solidity, came, town and gardens, out of his cup of tea.

You see, I believe that it is almost solely from involuntary memories that the artist ought to take the central substance of his work. First of all, precisely because they are involuntary, because they form themselves, attracted by the resemblance of an identical moment, they alone have the stamp of authenticity. Also, they bring things back to us in an exactly right dosage of memory and forgetfulness. And finally, as they make us experience the same sensation in a completely different circumstance, they liberate it from all contingency, they give us its extra-temporal essence, that which is precisely the substance of the beautiful style, that general and necessary truth which the beauty of the style alone translates.

If I permit myself to meditate this way on my book, it is not because it is in any way a work of mediation, but because its slightest elements were supplied to me by my sensibility, because I first perceived them at my very depths, without understanding them, having as much trouble in converting them into something intelligible as if they had been as foreign to the world of intelligence as—what shall I say?—a musical *motif*. You probably believe this is all a matter of subtleties, but I assure you, these are, quite the contrary, realities. What we did not have to explain to ourselves, what was previously clear (for example, logical concepts), does not really belong to us, we do not even know if it is the real. It belongs to the "possible" that we choose arbitrarily. Besides, you know, this becomes evident at once in the style.

Style is in no way a decoration as some people believe; it is not even a matter of technique; it is—as color is with painters—a quality of vision, the revelation of the particular universe which each of us sees, and which others do not see. The pleasure that an artist gives us is to make us know one universe more.

The Vocation of the Artist

MARCEL PROUST

The idea of a popular art, like that of a patriotic art, seemed to me ridiculous, even if it had not been dangerous. If it was a question of making art accessible to the people, the perfections of form, "good for the idle class," were sacrificed. Now, I had been among society folk enough to know that they, not the electrical workers, are the real illiterates. In this respect, an art popular in form would have been more properly designed for the members of the Jockey Club than the Confédération Général du Travail. As to subjects, the common people are carried away by popular novels just about as much as children are by the books written specially for them. In one's reading one seeks to get out of the ordinary environment, and workingmen are as much interested in princes as princes are in workingmen. At the very beginning of the war M. Barrès declared that the artist (in this case it was Titian) should first of all serve the glory of his country. But he can serve it only by being an artist or, in other words, on condition that when he is studying the laws of Art, making his experiments and his discoveries, as delicate as those of Science, he think of nothing—not even his country—except the truth that is before him. Let us not imitate the Revolutionists who out of "civic spirit" scorned, if they did not actually destroy, the works of Watteau and La Tour, painters who were a greater honor to France than all the artists of the Revolution. Anatomy is, perhaps,

Proust's *Le Temps Retrouvé* was first published by Librairie Gallimard, Paris, in 1927. Translated by Frederick A. Blossom as part of *The Past Recaptured*, Random House, Inc., N. Y., 1932, pp. 216-230. The text of this selection has been revised in accordance with that of *A la Recherche du Temps Perdu*, Bibliothèque de la Pléiade, Librairie Gallimard, Paris, 1954, t. III, pp. 888-899.

not what a tender-hearted person would select if he had the choice. It was not out of the kindness of his virtuous heart— and he was very kind—that Choderlos de Laclos wrote *Les Liaisons Dangereuses,* nor because of his liking for the *petite bourgeoisie*—or the *grande,* either—that Flaubert selected for subjects those of *Madame Bovary* and *L'Education Sentimentale.* Some said that the art of a period of hurry would be concise— just as others predicted before the war that it would not last long. In like manner the railroad was to kill meditation, it was useless to long for the days of stage-coaches; but the automobile performs their functions and again sets the tourists down near the abandoned churches.

An image presented by life brings us in reality at that moment multiple and varying sensations. For example, the sight of the cover of a book one has previously read retains, woven into the letters of its title, the moonbeams of a far-off summer night. The fragrance of the morning cup of coffee brings us that vague hope of fair weather which so often in former years smiled at us in the bright uncertainty of early day as we drank our coffee from a bowl of creamy white china, crinkled like coagulated milk. An hour is not merely an hour. It is a vase filled with per- fumes, sounds, plans and climates. What we call reality is a cer- tain relationship between these sensations and the memories which surround us at the same time (a relationship that is de- stroyed by a bare cinematographic presentation, which gets fur- ther away from the truth the more closely it claims to adhere to it) the only true relationship, which the writer must recapture so that he may forever link together in his phrase its two distinct elements. One may list in an interminable description the objects that figured in the place described, but truth will begin only when the writer takes two different objects, establishes their relation- ship—analogous in the world of art to the sole relationship in the world of science, the law of cause and effect—and encloses them in the necessary rings of a beautiful style, or even when, like life itself, comparing similar qualities in two sensations, he makes their essential nature stand out clearly by joining them in a metaphor, in order to remove them from the contingencies of time. . . . From this point of view regarding the true path of art, was not nature herself a beginning of art, she who had often allowed me to know the beauty of something only a long time afterwards and only through something else—midday at Combray through the sound of its bells, the morning at Doncières through the hiccoughs of our hot-water furnace? The relationship may be uninteresting, the objects mediocre and the style bad, but without that relationship there is nothing. . . .

But there was more than that, I reflected. If reality were merely that by-product of existence, so to speak, approximately identical for everybody—because, when we say "bad weather, war, cab-stand, brightly lighted restaurant, garden in bloom," everyone knows what we mean—if reality were that, then naturally a sort of cinematographic film of these things would be enough and the "style" or the "literature" that departed from their simple theme would be an artificial *hors d'œuvre*. But was that truly reality? If I tried to analyze for myself just what takes place in us at the moment when something makes a certain impression on us—as, for example, that day when, as I crossed the bridge over the Vivonne, the shadow of a cloud on the water made me exclaim, "Zut alors!" as I leaped for joy; or when, as I listened to a remark of Bergotte's, all that I caught of my impression was this, which was not particularly appropriate to him: "It's very fine"; or when, irritated by some discourtesy, Bloch uttered these words, not at all suited to such a vulgar experience: "It is simply incredible that anyone would behave that way"; or when, flattered at having been cordially received at the Guermantes' and, besides, a bit flustered by their wines, I could not keep from saying to myself half aloud as I left them, "Just the same, they're charming people, with whom it would be delightful to pass one's life"—I perceived that, to describe these impressions, to write that essential book, the only true book, a great writer does not need to invent it, in the current sense of the term, since it already exists in each one of us, but merely to translate it. The duty and the task of a writer are those of translator.

Now while, in cases involving the inaccurate language of injured pride for example, the straightening out of the oblique inner discourse (which diverges farther and farther from the first central impression), until it coincides with the straight line that should have started from the impression, is an arduous process against which our indolence sets up a sullen resistance, there are other cases—where love is involved, for instance—in which this operation becomes positively painful. All our feigned indifference, our indignation against the very natural falsehoods—so like those we resort to ourselves—in a word, all that we have said again and again whenever we were unhappy or betrayed, not only to the beloved one but even, while waiting to see her, continually to ourselves and sometimes even aloud, breaking the silence of our bedroom with such phrases as, "No, really, such conduct is intolerable," or "I have consented to see you again, but for the last time, and I will not deny that it makes me very sad"—to bring all that back to the truth, based on what we really felt and from which it has wandered so far, means doing away with all that we clung to most strongly, all that formed the content of our impassioned conversations face to face with ourselves, in the midst of feverish plans for letters and other steps to be taken.

Even in our artistic enjoyment, although sought after for the impressions it gives, we are very quickly content to leave those impressions aside as something that cannot be expressed and confine our attention to those phases which allow us to experience the pleasure without analyzing the sensations thoroughly, while thinking that we are communicating them to others with similar tastes, with whom we shall be able to converse because we shall be talking to them of something which is the same for them as for us, the personal root of our own impression having been eliminated. At the very times when we are the most dispassionate observers of nature, of society, love, even art itself, since every impression has two parts, one of them incorporated in the object and the other prolonged within ourselves and therefore knowable only to us, we are quick to neglect the latter, that is to say, the one part to which we ought to devote our attention, and consider only the other half, which, being outside ourselves, cannot be studied deeply and consequently never will cause us any fatiguing exertion; the slight groove that a musical phrase or the sight of a church made in our consciousness we find it too difficult to try to comprehend. But we play the symphony again and again or keep returning to look at the church, until, in this running away from our own life which we have not the courage to face—they call this "erudition"—we come to know them as well, and in the same manner, as the most learned lover of music or archeology. How many there are, consequently, who stop at that point and extract nothing from their impression, but go to their graves useless and unsatisfied, like celibates of art. They are tormented by the same regrets as virgins and idlers, regrets that fecund labor would dispel. They are more wrought up over works of art than the real artists, because they do not labor arduously to get to the bottom of their emotional state and therefore it is diffused in outward expression, puts heat into their remarks and blood into their faces; they think they are doing something really great when, after the execution of a work they like, they shout vociferously "Bravo, bravo!" But these manifestations do not force them to seek light on the nature of their love; they do not know what it really is. Meanwhile, this unexpended passion exuberates into even their calmest conversation and leads them to indulge in grand gestures, facial contortions and noddings of the head when they talk of art. "I have been at a concert where they played some music which, I admit, did not thrill me. Then the quartet began and, *nom d'une pipe*, that was another story!" (Here the music lover's face assumes an anxious expression, as if he were saying to himself, "Why, I see sparks, I smell something burning; there must be a fire somewhere!") "Good Lord! what a difference! It was exasperating, it was badly written, but it was stunning! It was not something everybody could appreciate." And yet, ridiculous though these devotees may be, they are not entirely to be scorned. They are nature's first efforts in the process of evolving the artist; they are as shapeless and lacking in viability as the earliest animals, which preceded the present species and were not so constituted as to be able to survive. These weak-willed, sterile dabblers should arouse our sympathy like those first contrivances which were not able to leave the ground, but in which there was, not yet the means, secret and still to be discovered, but at any rate the desire, to fly. "And let me tell you, old man," adds the dilettante, as he takes your arm, "that's the eighth time I've heard it and I promise you, it won't be the last." And in truth, since they fail to assimilate the really nourishing part of art, they suffer from a continual need of artistic enjoyment, a gnawing hunger that nothing can satisfy. So they go and applaud the same work for a long time at a stretch, believing also that in being present they are performing a duty, an act of piety, as others regard their attendance at a meeting of a Board of Directors or a funeral. Then come works of a different, even quite contrary, character in literature, painting, or music. For the ability to launch new ideas and systems and, especially, to absorb them has always been much more widespread than genuine good taste, even among the producers of art, and this tendency is spreading considerably with the increase in the number of literary reviews and journals—and, along with them, of people who imagine they have been called to be writers and artists. There was a time, for example, when the better element of our youth, the more intelligent and more disinterested, no longer cared for any but works having a lofty moral and sociological, even religious significance. They had the idea that that was the criterion of the value of a work, thereby repeating the error of such as David, Chenavard, Brunetière, and others. Instead of Bergotte, whose airiest sentences, as a matter of fact, required much profound meditation, they preferred writers who seemed more profound only because they did not write as well. "His intricate way of writing is suited only to society people," the democratically minded said, thereby paying society folk a compliment they did not deserve. But the moment our reasoning intelligence tries to judge works of art, there is no longer anything fixed or certain; one can prove anything one wishes to. Whereas the real essence of talent is a gift, an attribute of a cosmic character, the presence of which should first of all be sought for underneath the surface fashions of thought and style, it is by these latter qualities that the critics classify an author. Because of his peremptory tone and his ostentatious scorn of the school that preceded him, they put the mantle of prophecy on a writer who has no new message to deliver. This constant aberration of the critics is such that a writer should almost prefer to be judged by the public at large (if the latter were not incapable even of understanding what an artist has attempted in a line of effort unfamiliar to it). For the talent of a great writer—which, after all, is merely an instinct religiously hearkened to (while silence is imposed on everything else) perfected and understood—has more in common with the instinctive life of the people than with the superficial verbiage and fluctuating standards of the conventionally recognized judges. Their battle of words begins all over again every ten years—for the kaleidoscope comprises not only society groups, but also social, political and religious ideas, which temporarily spread out more broadly through refraction in the large masses but nevertheless are short-lived, like all ideas whose novelty succeeds in deceiving only minds that are not very exacting as to proofs. Therefore parties and schools have followed one another, attracting to themselves always the same minds, men of only relative intelligence, always prone to partisan enthusiasms which less credulous minds, more exacting in the matter of proofs, avoid. Unfortunately the former, just because they are only half-wits, need to round out their personalities with action; therefore they are more active than the superior minds, attract the crowd and build up around themselves, not only exaggerated reputations for some, and unwarranted condemnation of others, but civil and foreign wars, which it ought to be possible to escape with a little non-royalist self-criticism.

And as for the pleasure that a perfectly balanced mind, a heart that is truly alive finds in the beautiful thought of some master, it is no doubt wholly sound, but however precious may be the men who are capable of enjoying it (how many are there in twenty years?) it nevertheless reduces them to the condition of being merely the full consciousness of someone else. When a man has done everything to win the love of a woman who could only have made him unhappy and, despite repeated efforts over many years, he has not even been able to obtain a rendezvous with her, instead of trying to describe his sufferings and the danger he has escaped, he reads and rereads this *pensée* from La Bruyère, annotating it with "a million words" and the most moving memories of his own life: "Men often want to love and do not know how to succeed in so doing; they seek defeat but are not able to find it, so that, if I may so express it, they are forced to remain free." Whether he who wrote that *pensée* intended it so or not (and then it should read "be loved," instead of "love," and it would be finer that way) it is certain that the sensitive man of letters referred to gives it life, fills it with meaning to the point of bursting and cannot repeat it without overflowing with joy to find it so true and beautiful, and yet he has added hardly anything to it and there remains merely the *pensée* of La Bruyère.

How could documentary realism have any value at all, since it is underneath little details such as it notes down that reality is hidden—the grandeur in the distant sound of an airplane or in the lines of the spires of Saint-Hilaire, the past contained in the savor of a *madeleine,* and so forth—and they have no meaning if one does not extract it from them. Stored up little by little in our memory, it is the chain of all the inaccurate impressions, in which there is nothing left of what we really experienced, which constitutes for us our thoughts, our life, reality, and a so-called "art taken from life" would simply reproduce that lie, an art as thin and poor as life itself, without any beauty, a repetition of what our eyes see and our intelligence notes, so wearisome and futile that one is at a loss to understand where the artist who devotes himself to that finds the joyous, energizing spark that can stimulate him to activity and enable him to go forward with his task. The grandeur of real art, on the contrary, art that M. de Norpois would have called "a pastime for dilettanti," is to rediscover, grasp again and lay before us that reality from which we live so far removed and from which we become more and more separated as the formal knowledge which we substitute for it grows in thickness and imperviousness—that reality which there is grave danger we might die without ever having known and yet which is simply our life. Life as it really is, life disclosed at last and made clear, consequently the only life that is really lived is literature; that life which in one sense is to be found at every moment in every man, as well as in the artist. But men fail to see it because they do not try to get light on it. And thus their past is encumbered with countless photographic negatives which lie there useless because the intelligence has not "developed" them. To grasp again our life—and also the life of others; for style is for the writer, as for the painter, a question, not of technique but of vision. It is the revelation—impossible by direct and conscious means—of the qualitative differences in the way the world appears to us, differences which, but for art, would remain the eternal secret of each of us. Only by art can we get outside ourselves, know what another sees of this universe, which is not the same as ours and the different views of which would otherwise have remained as unknown to us as those there may be on the moon. Thanks to art, instead of seeing only one world, our own, we see it under multiple forms, and as many as there are original artists, just so many worlds have we at our disposal, differing more widely from one another than those that roll through infinite space, and years after the glowing center from which they emanated has been extinguished, be it called Rembrandt or Vermeer, they continue to send us their own rays of light.

This work of the artist, to seek to discern something different underneath material, experience, words, is exactly the reverse of the process which, during every minute that we live with our attention diverted from ourselves, is being carried on within us by pride, passion, intelligence and also by our habits, when they hide our true impressions from us by burying them under the mass of nomenclatures and practical aims which we erroneously call life. After all, that art, although so complicated, is actually the only living art. It alone expresses to others and discloses to us our own life, that life which cannot be "observed" and the visible manifestations of which need to be translated and often read backwards and deciphered with much effort. But all the work of our pride, our passion, our imitative spirit, our abstract intelligence, art will undo and will make us retrace our steps and return to the depths of our own selves, where what has really existed lies unknown to us. And it is, indeed, alluring, this task of re-creating the true life and reviving the youthful freshness of our impressions, but it calls for courage of every sort—even sentimental—for it means, first of all, giving up our dearest illusions, ceasing to believe in the objectivity of what we have ourselves built up, and instead of lulling ourselves for the hundredth time with the words, "She was very sweet," reading behind all this, "I enjoyed having her in my embrace." It is true, what I experienced in those hours of love, all men undergo likewise. One goes through an experience, but what one has felt is like these negatives which show nothing but black until they have been held up before a lamp and they, too, must be looked at from the reverse side; one has no idea what they contain until they have been held up before the intelligence, and only when it has thrown light upon them and intellectualized them do we distinguish—and with what effort!—the outline of what we have felt.

But I also realized that the suffering I had at first undergone with Gilberte at the thought that our love does not belong to the one who inspires it, is incidentally salutary as a means to an end (for, however short our life is to be, it is only while we are suffering that our thoughts, as though stirred by perpetual, changing movements, bring up within our range of vision, as in a storm, all that boundless world, governed by laws, but of which we had no view from our ill-placed window, for the calm of happiness leaves it all too smooth and below our range of vision; perhaps only in a few great geniuses does this movement constantly go on without their having need to be stirred by suffering; and yet, perhaps, when we study the abundant and regular development of their joyous work, we are too much inclined to infer that their lives were joyful also, whereas, on the contrary, they may have been continually filled with sorrow). But the principal reason is: if we do not love solely a Gilberte (that which made us suffer so keenly) it is not because we loved also an Albertine, but because our love is a portion of our soul more lasting than the various selves which die successively in us and which would selfishly like to retain this love—a portion of our soul which, regardless of the useful suffering this may cause us, must detach itself from its human objects in order to restore its quality of generality and give this love, an understanding of this love, to all the world, to the universal intelligence, and not first to this woman, then to that, in whom this one and that of our successive selves seek to lose their identity.

My task, then, I reflected, was to re-establish the significance of even the slightest signs by which I was surrounded (the Guermantes, Albertine, Gilberte, Saint-Loup, Balbec and so forth), long familiarity having destroyed their meaning for me. We have to bear in mind that when we shall have attained reality, we shall not be able to express it and preserve it for all time unless we put aside all that is different from it and is being continually suggested to us by the haste that comes from habit. More than anything else, I would exclude, therefore, all those remarks that come from the lips rather than the mind, clever remarks such as one makes in conversation and which, after a long conversation with others, one continues to utter in imaginary discussions with oneself, so that they fill the mind with lies, those entirely mechanical remarks which any writer who so lowers himself as to use them accompanies with a little smile, a little grimace such as constantly disfigures the spoken phrase of a Sainte-Beuve, for example, whereas real books must be the product, not of broad daylight and small talk but of darkness and silence. And since art is a faithful re-composing of life, around the verities which one has finally found within oneself there will always float an atmosphere of poetry, the sweetness of mystery which is only the last traces of the semi-darkness we have had to pass through, the measure of the profundity of a work of art, indicated with precision as by a depth gauge. (For this profundity is not inherent in certain subjects, as some materialistically spiritualist novelists believe because they themselves cannot go below the world of outward appearances, and all their noble intentions, like the virtuous harangues characteristic of certain people incapable of the slightest kindly effort, should not blind us to the fact that they have not had strength of mind enough even to rid themselves of all the hackneyed forms acquired by imitation).

As for the truths which the intelligence—even that of the finest minds—garners right out in the open, lying before it in broad daylight, their value may be very great, but they have harsher outlines and are all on the surface, with no depth, because no depths had to be penetrated in order to get to them and they have not been re-created. Often writers in whom one no longer discerns these mysterious truths, after a certain age write only with their intelligence, which has acquired more and more power; for this reason the books of their mature period have more force than those of their youth, but no longer the same velvety smoothness.

And yet I felt that these truths which the intelligence draws directly from reality are not entirely to be scorned, for it may be that they fix, in a grosser substance, it is true, but nevertheless pierce with understanding, those impressions which are brought to us, outside of all considerations of time, by the essential qualities common to sensations of the past and present, but which, being more precious, are too rare for the work of art to be composed wholly of them. I felt surging within me a multitude of truths concerning passions,[1] characters and customs which might well serve in that manner. . . . The perception of these truths brought me joy, and yet I seemed to remember that more than one of them I had discovered through suffering

1. Every person who makes us suffer we can associate with a divinity, of which that person is only a fragmentary reflection—the lowest step of the approach to the temple, as it were—and the contemplation of this divinity as a pure idea gives us instant joy in place of the sorrow we were suffering; the entire art of living consists in making use of those who cause us suffering only as so many steps enabling us to draw nearer to its divine form and thus daily people our life with divinities.

and others in the midst of very commonplace pleasures. And then a new light dawned within me, less brilliant, it is true, than the one which had disclosed to me that the work of art is our only means of recapturing lost Time. And I understood that all these materials for literary work were nothing else than my past life and that they had come to me in the midst of frivolous pleasures, in idleness, through tender affection and through sorrow, and that I had stored them up without foreseeing their final purpose or even their survival, any more than does the seed when it lays by all the sustenance that is going to nourish the seedling. Like the seed, I might die as soon as the plant had been formed, and I found that I had been living for this seedling without knowing it, without any indication whatsoever that my life would ever witness the realization of those books I so longed to write but for which I used to find no subject when I sat down at my table. And so my entire life up to that day could—and, from another point of view, could not—be summed up under the title, *A Vocation*. It could not, in the sense that literature had not played any part in my life as yet. But it could, on the other hand, in that my life, the memories of its sorrows and its joys, constituted a reserve after the manner of the albumen stored in the ovule of plants, from which it draws its nutrition in order to develop into a seed, long before there is anything to show that the embryo of a plant is developing, although it is the repository of secret but very active chemical and respiratory phenomena. Thus my life was in contact with the forces that would bring about its maturation.

The Art of the Novel

THOMAS MANN

I am going to speak to you for the next few days about the art of the novel. Now I can well imagine a person who might deny that the novel is even an art form at all. "To be sure, one assigns the novel," such an aesthetician would say, "to epic literature, a main division of poetry, which, besides the real heroic epic poem, the popular epic derived from the legendary sagas, and the individual art-epic, also comprises the great epic, the idyl and legend, the ballad and romance, the folk-tale and, finally, also the novel and the short story. But first of all," (I am still letting this strict aesthetician speak) "the epic art form ranks, in general, in second place: it is not the peer of the drama, which combines within itself all the remaining genres of literature and is actually the apex of poetry and a queen in her own right. And, in the second place, the prose novel is an inferior and, from the formal point of view, very undignified, dissolute form of the verse-epic and the novelist is only a half-brother of the poet, an illegitimate son of poetry."

So much for the academic aesthetician. One listens to him with due respect, although one cannot suppress one or another objection, both against his first statement and his second. It is and remains the most idle and most doctrinaire of undertakings to set up any order of rank whatsoever as a principle in the realm of the types and genres of art. As foolish as it would be to elevate one single form of artistic manifestation: music, for example, or painting, or poetry as the highest and noblest form over the

"Die Kunst des Romans" is the text of a lecture delivered by Thomas Mann at Princeton University in 1939. It is printed in *Altes und Neues*, S. Fischer Verlag, Frankfurt, 1953, pp. 387-401. Translated by Herman Salinger.

others (for reasons which might have their points but which could be as well advanced for the elevation and coronation of any of the other arts), just so lacking in taste is it to set up, within one single sphere of creativity, namely literature, an order or rank of forms and genres. The basic pre-eminence of, let us say, the drama over narrative literature may so easily be questioned that at this point one finds oneself tempted to fall into the same error and to reverse the order of rank. Perhaps the epic spirit, which moreover is capable of comprising the lyric and the dramatic elements, the same way that the epic and the lyric may be included within the drama—perhaps, I say, the spirit of the narrative, the "Eternally Homeric," this world-wide, worldly-wise, enunciatory spirit of creation of the past, perhaps this spirit is the most venerable embodiment of the poetic and therefore the narrator, this whispering conjuror and invoker of the imperfect tense, its most worthy representative. The narrative Vedas of India were also called *Itihasa-Hymns* after the expression *"Iti ha asa,"* meaning "thus it was." Perhaps this "thus it was" is a more solemn poetic attitude than the "here it is" of the drama. But these are objectively unanswerable questions, questions of temperament and taste; and, in the case of artistic genres, everything depends solely on the art and not on the genre.

The second argument against the prose novel is doubtless a little stronger: that it is a decadent form of the "real" epic, that is, of the verse epic. True enough, historically, the novel regularly signifies a later, less naive, so-to-speak "more modern" stage in the epic life of peoples, and in comparison with the novel, the epic always represents something like the good old classical age. It starts off as something hymnic and hieratic and then becomes realistic-democratic. At times even this popular, entertaining level exists directly alongside the solemn plane of expression, as in Egypt, where the period of the sixth dynasty already produces such prose as the famous *Adventures of Sinuhe,* after which the novel of the shipwrecked man, the story of the eloquent peasant, the tale of the two brothers follow, probably forming the model of the biblical Joseph story, and then *The Treasure of Rhampsinit*—all of these are matters from which one can learn much more about old Egypt than from all the official hymnologies of the gods. In India we first have the virtually sacred *Mahabharata* with its hundred thousand double verses, and then the Indian novel, which has the effect of a luxuriantly vegetating, fantastically unbridled and linguistically wild variation of it. In the land of Homer, it is Hellenism and Alexandrianism which first favor the prose novel. Thus the genesis of the travel novel of *The Wonders Beyond Thule*, which is merely a late reflection of *The Odyssey;* and we have Parthenios who, with his book *On the Adventures of Love*, founded the prose love-novel. Here we have such unrestrained and boundless adventures as the *Story of Leukippe and Kleitophon* by Achilleus Tatios of Alexandria. But we also have at this time Aesop's *Fables*, which have become a part of the cultural possessions of all nations, affecting the medieval *fabliaux* and again taking the form of the poetic epic in Goethe's *Reineke Fuchs*—"Reynard the Fox." In Rome, the heroic cantos of Virgil come first, and only after him the contemporary novel of Petronius and then *The Golden Ass of Apuleius*, which, to be sure, is a gem of the world's novelistic literature and includes the charming tale of Cupid and Psyche. There is no doubt that in Persia a novelistic literature of loquacious wisdom and variety follows only on the heels of the classical epic of a Nisami and a Firdusi as a product of dissolution; but in any case it produces *The Parrot Book*, a framed collection of fifty-two erotic stories, which is the forerunner of *The Decameron* and of the narratives of Bandello. Again leading directly into the novel we find the French heroic epic. First comes *The Song of Roland* and then the prose of *Lancelot*, a novel, of which aside from the title we know only the name of the author: Arnaut Daniel. The book itself has been lost and yet it lives on in a ghostly-famous manner in world literature. It is indeed in all probability, the book in which Dante's Paolo and Francesca were reading together—up to a certain point, where it is said: "That day they read no further." An interesting case: that a prose novel is taken up as a motif into the action of the high epic and there celebrated!

Let us stay for one moment with Dante. He is a singer, not a narrator. One would find it unsuitable to call *The Divine*

Comedy a novel. But what is the lexical definition of the novel? Whence comes the name, the word that even in English is not always called "novel" or "fiction" but sometimes "romance," as in the German "*Roman*," in the French "*roman*," in the Italian "*romanzo*"? Originally it simply meant a narrative work which was composed among a Romanic people *in the popular language*. Now, *The Divine Comedy* fulfills this condition: it is composed in the *lingua parlata*, not in Latin; in this sense it is a popular work, accessible to the people; in this respect, it makes its exit out of the Middle Ages and directly into the modern period—this sacred epic, the source book of today's Italian, is in the literal sense of the word a "*romanzo*," a novel.

But let us proceed. The Arthurian stories consist of a breaking down into prose of the Anglo-Norman heroic poem, the Grail epic. But in the fourteenth century these novels of the French Arthurian cycle, the novels of the Round Table, penetrate into Spain, and the *Amadis of Gaul* is of their type—the prototype of those chivalric novels which turned the head of Cervantes' Don Quixote. Out of an originally purely satirical purpose directed against the idealist-heroic chivalric fiction grows a national and a world book, a novel, which no one hesitates to name in the same breath alongside the highest products of poetic genius, with Shakespeare and Goethe. Here we stand facing a creative phenomenon in which the theoretic and aesthetic differences in rank between epic and novel are completely obliterated and the essence of the eternally-epic itself, no matter whether sung or spoken, whether verse or prose, reveals itself in its unity and independence. If *The Divine Comedy* is a novel, if *The Odyssey* was one, then *Don Quixote* is an epic, and, to be sure, one of the greatest. The art *form* becomes a matter of indifference whenever the genius of the art *genre* itself emerges in all its sovereignty and independent greatness.

Permit me the personal and unacademic confession that my love and my interest belong to that very art genre, to the *genius of the epic* itself, and forgive me if a lecture on "the art of the novel" turns, in spite of myself, into praise of the spirit of epic art. It is a powerful and majestic spirit, expansive, rich in life, as wide as the sea in its rolling motion, at once grandiose and exact, melodic and circumspect; it does not aim at the excerpt, the episode, it wants the whole, the world with all its countless episodes and details on which it tarries, forgetful of self, as though each one of them were of special concern. For the novel is not in a hurry, it has infinite time, it is the spirit of patience, of loyalty, of endurance, of slowness which love renders enjoyable, the spirit of enchanting tedium. The novel scarcely knows how to begin except with the very beginning of all things and does not want to end at all; for the novel, the poet's line holds true: "The fact that you cannot end is what makes you great." But its greatness is mild, restful, serene, wise—"objective." It keeps its distance from things, *has* by its very nature distance from them; it hovers over them and smiles down upon them, regardless of how much, at the same time, it involves the hearer or reader in them by a process of weblike entanglement. The art of the epic is "Apollinian" art as the aesthetic term would have it; because Apollo, distant marksman, is the god of distance, of objectivity, the god of irony. Objectivity is irony and the spirit of epic art is the spirit of irony.

Here you will be startled and will ask yourselves: how is that? Objectivity and irony—what have they to do with one another? Isn't irony the opposite of objectivity? Isn't it a highly subjective attitude, the ingredient of a romantic libertinism, which contrasts with classic repose and objectivity as their opposite? That is correct. Irony can have this meaning. But I use the word here in a broader, larger sense, given it by romantic subjectivism. In its equanimity it is an almost monstrous sense: the sense of *art* itself, a universal affirmation, which, as such, is also a universal negation; an all-embracing crystal clear and serene glance, which is the very glance of art itself, that is to say: a glance of the utmost freedom and calm and of an objectivity untroubled by any moralism. This was the glance of Goethe who was to that extent an artist that he uttered the strange and unforgettable characterization of irony: "Irony is that little grain of salt which alone renders the dish palatable." Not for nothing did he remain all his life such a great admirer of Shakespeare; for in the dramatic cosmos of Shakespeare this cosmic irony of art actually prevails, rendering his work so objectionable to such a moralist as Tolstoi took pains to be. I speak of this cosmic irony of art when I speak of the ironic objectivity of the epic. In all of this you must not think of coldness and lovelessness, contempt and scorn. Epic irony is rather an irony of the heart, a loving irony; it is greatness filled with tenderness for little things.

The Persian poet Firdusi, about the year 1000 A.D., wrote the epic *Shah-nameh*, "the King's Book," a renewal of the Persian royal legend. For twenty-two years he worked on it in the land of Thus. He was fifty-eight when he came to Glazna to the Sultan, who offered him a thousand gold pieces for every thousand couplets of the long poem. Firdusi, however, said: "I do not wish to be paid until I am finished." Decades passed before he was finished, and according to his own feelings, his own aims, he surely never did finish. He sat there and wove the giant carpet of his poem, full of figures, stories, adventures, heroic deeds, demonic magic, and colorful arabesques. He grew to be eighty years old at the task. Then he declared his work finished. It was eight times as long as *The Iliad* and added up to sixty thousand couplets. The Sultan cheated him, sending him for each thousand of them not a thousand gold pieces, but a thousand pieces of silver. The old man was sitting in his bath when the honorarium arrived. He gave it to the messenger who brought it and to the bath servants, as a tip.

This is an anecdote from the world of epic, a magnificent anecdote. There are none of this sort in the world of the drama or the lyric, which are worlds short of breath, quickly finished in comparison. The epic work, *une mer à boire*, a miraculous undertaking, in which must be invested masses of life, sincere artistic industry and a long-suffering loyalty which renews its inspiration every day—with its gigantic "miniaturism" which seems to be insistent about detail as though it meant everything, and yet at the same time can keep its eye unswervingly on the whole—this is what I have in mind in sepaking to you about "the art of the novel." In so doing I have had to think of Firdusi and his fabulous royal epic and also the fact that he gave away his honorarium because they paid him for his verses in silver instead of gold. And even if they had been lines of prose he would have —if I know him aright—refused to accept silver for gold. I neither can nor wish to feel any difference in essence or in rank between the epic and the novel, between *The Divine Comedy* and *The Human Comedy*, and I find it splendid that Balzac gave his novelistic edifice a name which unites these two spheres and asserts their equality of birth.

Another creative writer of modern novels was Leo Tolstoi— probably the mightiest of them all. His is one of those cases which tempt us to reverse what the academic aestheticians put forward as the relationship between novel and epic and to think of the novel not as a decadent form of the epic, but to see in the epic a primitive prototype of the novel.

This is a thoroughly possible viewpoint, historically speaking; for, taking it all in all, there is something peculiar about the phenomenon of dissolution and decay, about so-called degeneration. It is, generally speaking, a complicated problem, a problem of intellectual biology, which is not simply identical with natural biology. In the intellectual realm dissolution and decay may become empty words or words which signify the very opposite of what they are intended to mean in their purely natural biological sense. Insofar as they indicate a later stage, they also indicate a higher, more developed one. "Decay" can signify a refining, a deepening, an ennobling. It need have nothing to do with death and finality; on the contrary, it can be intensification, elevation, perfection of life.

It is possible and perhaps it is advisable to see the novel and the epic in such a relationship. The one is a modern, the other an archaic world. The verse epic bears, in our eyes, an archaic stamp—as the verse itself is intrinsically archaic and actually still belongs to a world of magic. The epics of early times were neither read nor told; they were surely a sing-song accompanied by a stringed instrument; the name of "singer"—which remained the poet's name in archaic or pseudo-archaic language— was for a long while, down into the Middle Ages and the contests of the Minnesingers, literally accurate, and especially was the epic a kind of announcing song, and Father Homer, a blind singer—which does not prevent the "cantos" of the *Iliad* and *Odyssey*, as we know them, and likewise the *Edda* and the *Nibelungen-Lied* from being late literary versions of these original rhapsodies.

It would be a bold observation to say without further ado that the step to the prose novel clearly signified a heightening and a refinement of the lifeblood of the story. In the first place, the novel was actually an intricate and arbitrarily extravagant elaboration of the more strictly formed verse-epic. But it had possibilities within it, whose realization on its long course of development from the late Greek and Indian fabulous monsters down to the *Education Sentimentale* and the *Elective Affinities* entitles us to see in the epic merely an archaic forerunner of the novel.

The principle, however, which permitted the novel to travel this humanly significant path, is the principle of *subjectivization*. The German philosopher, Arthur Schopenhauer, who stood on a more intimate footing with art than is usual with most thinkers, has expressed this most effectively: "A novel will be all the higher and nobler in kind, in direct proportion to how much it presents inner and how little outer life; and this ratio will accompany all gradations of the novel, as a characteristic sign, from *Tristram Shandy* on down to the crudest and most adventurous chivalresque and gothic novel. *Tristram Shandy*, to be sure, has practically no action at all; but how very little has the *Nouvelle Héloïse*, and the same is true of *Wilhelm Meister!* Even *Don Quixote* has relatively little action and what there is is rather insignificant and humorous in its intent. And these four novels are the crowning glory of the species. Moreover, observe the wonderful novels of Jean Paul and see how much inner life they allow to move and have its being upon the narrowest external foundation. Even the novels of Walter Scott contain a significant overbalance of the inner over the outer life, and, in fact, the latter makes its appearance only for the purpose of setting the former into motion, whereas in bad novels it is there for its own sake. The art consists in employing the smallest possible amount of outer life in order to set the inner into the most violent motion; for the inner is actually the object of our interest. The task of the novelist is not to narrate great events but to make small ones interesting."

These are classic words and the final aphorism has always especially pleased me, dealing as it does with *making interesting*. The secret or mystery of the telling—for one can well speak of a secret—is to make something interesting which actually ought to be boring. It would be quite hopeless to try to open up and explain this secret. But it is not a matter of chance that Schopenhauer's pointed remark about making the small things interesting follows immediately on the heels of his observations about the *subjectivization* of the narrative art. The principle of subjectivization must play a role in that secret, so that we breathlessly hearken to that which is in and of itself insignificant and in so doing completely forget our liking for the coarsely exciting and robustly adventurous.

When the prose novel broke away from the epic, the narrative entered upon a path of development toward subjectivization and refinement: a long path, at the start of which this tendency was not yet suspected. To choose an example nationally close to me: what else is the German educational and developmental novel, what else is Goethe's *Wilhelm Meister*, but the subjectivization and sublimation of the adventure novel? How very much it is a question, in this subjectivization, of elevating the small and simple to a spiritual plane, and how much it revolves around reducing poetry to a bourgeois plane. This is to be seen with very great and instructive clarity in a critique which the romanticist Novalis, a seraphic poet, devoted to *Wilhelm Meister* and which is as malicious as it is accurate. Novalis did not care for this greatest German novel; he called it a *Candide, directed against poetry*. He found this book, regardless of its poetic manner of presentation, "unpoetic in the highest degree," a satire against poetry, religion, and so forth; a tasty dish, a holy idol made up out of straw and shavings. Back of it all he found nothing but farce. "Economical nature is true and lasting. In it the romantic, including nature poetry and the magical, goes to ruin.

It deals merely with usual human things; nature and mysticism are completely forgotten. It is a poetized bourgeois and domestic story. . . . The first book of *Meister* shows how pleasant even common daily events can sound, if they are presented in pleasing modulations, clothed simply in a cultivated and fluent style and walking past us at a good stride. . . ." "Goethe is a wholly *practical* poet," Novalis says elsewhere. "Goethe is in his works what the English are in their goods: highly simple, neat, comfortable, and lasting. He accomplished in German literature what Wedgwood did in the English art world; like the English, he has a naturally economical and noble taste, acquired through the understanding. . . . His inclination is rather to finish off something insignificant and to give it the highest polish and convenience, than to begin a world and to do something concerning which one knows in advance that he will never be able to carry it out completely."

One must know how to read the negative positively and must believe that malice can be fruitful and productive of understanding in order to prize this critique as much as I do. The aesthetic Anglicism that is ascribed to Goethe in it makes one think of the influence which the English middle-class novels of Richardson, Fielding, Goldsmith actually exercised on him. But it is the middle-class quality of the novel in general of which we become aware through the *Wilhelm Meister* critique of Novalis: its inborn democracy which differentiates it, both formally and in the history of ideas, from the feudalism of the epic and has made it the dominant art form of our epoch, the vessel of the modern soul. The astonishing flowering of the novel in Europe during the nineteenth century, in England, in France, in Russia, in the Scandinavian countries—this is no chance matter; it is connected with the contemporaneity and democracy of the novel, with its natural tendency to serve as an expression for modern life, with its social and psychological passion, which have made it into the representative art form of the age and the novelist, even the mediocre one, into the modern type of literary artist *par excellence*. This conception of the novelist as the most truly modern manifestation of the artist can be found in many places in

Nietzsche's cultural criticism: the modern novelist with his social and psychological curiosity and nervousness, his constitutional mixture of sensibility and sensitivity, his plastic and critical talents, this highly individuated instrument for the reception and communication of the most delicate sensations and ultimate events plays a distinguished role in Nietzsche's spiritual picture of his time—Nietzsche, who himself was a highly hybrid mixture of the artist and the seer, a kind of *"romancier"* who brought art and science closer together and allowed them to merge with each other more than did any spirit before him.

And here, expressly in regard to the novel and to its dominant position as the art form of our time, we must think of the significance to be allotted in general to the critical element: its significance for modern creativity and for the literary art work of the present. And again I must think of what the Russian philosopher Dmitri Merejkowski said *à propos* of Pushkin and Gogol about the displacement of pure *poetry* by *criticism*, the "transition from unconscious creation to *creative consciousness*." It is a question here of the same contrast which Schiller, in his famous essay, expresses in the formula of the "naive" and the "sentimental." What Merejkowski in the case of Gogol calls "criticism" or "creative consciousness" and what makes him— in comparison with the "unconscious creativity" of Pushkin— appear as the more modern, even the more future, is exactly what Schiller understands by the sentimental in contrast to the naive when he similarly explains the sentimental, the creativity of the consciousness and of criticism, as the newer, more modern stage of development.

This distinction belongs thoroughly to our theme: the characterization of the novel. The novel as a modern work of art represents that stage of "criticism" following the stage of "poetry." Its relation to the epic is the relation of the "creative consciousness" to "unconscious creativity." And it must be added that the novel as the democratic product of creative consciousness need by no means lag behind in *monumentality*.

The great social novel writing of Dickens, Thackeray, Tolstoi, Dostoievsky, Balzac, Zola, Proust is the real monumental art of the nineteenth century. These are English, Russian, French names —why is the German missing? The contribution of Germany to European narrative art is in some ways sublime: it consists chiefly of the novel of intellectual development like Goethe's *Wilhelm Meister* and later Gottfried Keller's *Der grüne Heinrich*. In addition we have, again from Goethe, a pearl of the world's novelistic art, *The Elective Affinities*, a psychological, scientific piece of prose fiction of the highest rank. Later, certain intellects of the unsuccessful bourgeois revolution of our country, representatives of "Young Germany," Immermann, Gutzkow, wrote social novels; they attracted little world interest and rightly did not penetrate into the European sphere. The novelistic prose of a Spielhagen is today so wilted that one may conclude it never was a true contribution to what we call the European novel. One must cite Theodore Fontane, among whose highly individualized late works at least one, *Effie Briest*, is a masterpiece of European proportions—without Europe or the world having especially bothered about him. Outside of Germany Fontane is practically unknown and already in South Germany and in Switzerland scarcely read. Not very different is the situation of the German-speaking Swiss: the powerful peasant moralist Gotthelf, who was very great in his art; the lovable Gottfried Keller, who wrote a prose which rang as true as gold and was a wonderful teller of modern tales; and Conrad Ferdinand Meyer, a historical novelist of the highest merit.

How does it happen that all of this does not really count on a European scale? And that one needs only to name one of the aforementioned western European and Russian names in order to feel the difference in influence and representative character? European influence, European representative character, the quality of world conquest that lies in those names of the great *romanciers*, is, in the case of Germany, to be found elsewhere than in literary-social criticism; namely, in music. The name which Germany has to counter that proud series of names, or to take its place alongside them, is Richard Wagner, whose work, to be sure, has much to do with the epic, but is musical drama. Germany's contribution to the monumental art of the nineteenth century is not of a literary but of a musical nature—and most characteristically so. The most remarkable common ground, from the point of view of the psychology of the age, could be shown to exist between the Wagnerian monumental work and the great European novelistic art of the nineteenth century. The *Ring of the Nibelungen* has much in common with the symbolic naturalism of Émile Zola's *Rougon-Macquart* series—even the use of the "leitmotif." But the essential and typical national difference is the social spirit of the French work, the mythically primitive poetic spirit of the German work. It would not be saying too much if one were to declare the novel of a truly European stamp to be actually foreign to Germany—in which something significant is expressed about the relationship of the German mind not only to the inborn democratic spirit of the novel as an art form, but to democracy generally, in the widest and most spiritual sense of the word.

When I speak of the foreignness of the novel in Germany and of the German novel in the world, I of course have the nineteenth century in mind and especially the second half; for the novel of the romantic period in Germany, to which Jean Paul, Novalis, Tieck, Schlegel, Arnim, and Brentano have made admirable contributions, has at least one representative, in E. T. A. Hoffmann, whose ghostly story-telling art has surely become European and has exercised a strong effect, especially in France. A similar influence on literary Europe is beginning today to emerge from the highly individual and significant narrative fiction of the short-lived German Czech, Franz Kafka, whose religious-humoristic dream-and-anxiety writings belong to the deepest and most remarkable products that world literature has brought forth in prose form. At the turn into the twentieth century and in its first third there takes place generally something like the formal and intellectual breakthrough of the German novel into the sphere of European interest. But of this, another time.

The Artist and Society

THOMAS MANN

The Artist and Society. I cannot help wondering whether it was realized what a touchy theme this is when it was assigned to us. I am afraid it was only too well realized and those responsible are only assuming an air of innocence. Why not say at once: "The Artist and Politics"—since after all, behind the word "society" the political stands hidden? It is very badly hidden behind it, because the artist as critic of society is already made political, is already the politicizing artist—or, in a word: the moralizing artist. In its full nomenclature the subject would have to run: "The Artist and *Morality*"—a very mischievous formulation of the problem and almost consciously calculated to get us into an embarrassing situation. Indeed, it must be obvious that the artist is originally not a moral being but an aesthetic one, that his basic drive is the play instinct, and not virtue; in fact, that he, in all his naiveté, dares to play, if even merely dialectically, with the problems and contradictions of morality.

I do not mean to disparage the artist when I delineate the looseness of his relationship to morality, hence to politics, and furthermore to the problem of society. I could not possibly blame that artist who might declare that world-betterment in a moral sense was not the affair of him or his kind. The artist, according to him, might "better" the world in quite another way than by moral precept; namely, by giving form and substance to his life—and, in a representative way, to life in general—through

"Der Künstler und die Gesellschaft" was first presented by Thomas Mann as a radio talk on the Third Programme of the British Broadcasting Corporation in June, 1952. The text, revised by the author, appears in *Altes und Neues*, S. Fischer Verlag, Frankfurt, 1953, pp. 433-442. Translated by Herman Salinger.

word, image, and thought, thus making the life phenomenon transparent for the thing Goethe called "the life's life": the spirit. I could not possibly contradict him when and if he insisted that *animation*, in every sense of the word, were the real mission of art—and nothing more. In Goethe, whom I am so fond of quoting because he has said the right thing in the most graceful way about most of the things of this world, one reads the following short and clear statement: "It may well be that a work of art has moral effects; but to demand moral aims and purposes from the artist means to botch his job for him." The word "job" has a peculiarly modest ring; and that modesty is involved in the artist's abhorrence of moralizing. This is made even clearer by another statement of Goethe's. As an old man he said: "It was never my way to declaim against institutions; *that always seemed to me to be presumptuous* and it may well be that I became polite too early in life. In short, it was never my way, and I have therefore always touched only the far end of the pole, gently." With this Goethe indicates clearly enough that moral, political, social criticism on the part of the artist is an overstepping of his boundaries, an offense against modesty. And should not modesty come to him naturally?

Modesty is natural to him, basically, not only in his relationship to reality and its "institutions" but also to art itself, which makes the individual artist in most cases feel very small. What puts his modesty into jeopardy is the peculiar tie between art and *criticism*, about which a word must be said here.

It is well known that very many artists are, at the same time, *judges* of the arts—art critics—or that they presume to be, one is almost tempted to say, in view of the contradiction that apparently lies in the circumstance of someone who feels himself to be very small before his particular form of art, and nevertheless does not hesitate to act as an expert judge of it. As a matter of fact, however, there is an element of criticism inborn and native to all art, indispensable to every form of disciplined productivity and therefore primarily a matter of self-discipline, yet very often equally inclined to turn itself outward and to indulge in critical aesthetics, to investigate and to evaluate from an aesthetic standpoint. Remarkable to say, it is in the sphere of the poetic, in the sphere of the art of literature, that this inclination expresses itself most frequently and reaches its strongest development. This is especially true in literature's apparently most delicate and most hesitant mode of being: *lyric poetry*. Lyric poetry is tied to criticism much more firmly than is the drama or the narrative form of art; this may be based upon the subjectivity of the lyric form, upon the lack of perspective in its utterance, upon its immediacy and the directness with which the word in a lyric poem is employed in the service of feeling, of mood, of view of life.

The word! Isn't criticism after all by its very nature an arrow from the bow of Apollo: whirring, *hitting* the target and left trembling, stuck in the black center? Even as song—indeed, especially as song—it is criticism: criticism of life, and as such never really convenient for the world. It will not surprise anyone if, in pursuing the question of the artist's relationship to society, I think first of all of the artist of the word, the artist in the person of the poet, the man of letters—and here it can be established that a certain opposition to reality, life, society, is inseparable from the existence of the writing artist, for the very reason that he is in league with the word. Actually, he develops from an early stage a feeling, composed of formal and intellectual elements, of superiority over the existing world, over bourgeois society; and the fact that his critical hostility toward the real and actual goes beyond the aesthetic and even lays claim to a certain moral quality, may appear most offensive and most lacking in modesty. Nevertheless it is true that something moral clings to the inborn critical quality of art and that this moral element obviously derives from the idea of "the Good" which is likewise at home in the realm of the aesthetic and of the ethical.

Good and evil—good and bad: Nietzsche made a great deal of psychological fuss with this pair of opposites, but it is a question whether bad and evil are really as different from each other as he wanted to show. In the aesthetic world, to be sure, the evil, the scornfully misanthropic and cruel, does not need to be the bad. Endowed with quality, it may be "good." But in the world of experience and of human society, the bad, the stupid and the false is also the evil; namely, that which is unworthy, and ruinous to mankind, and as soon as the critical side of art is turned toward the outside, as soon as it becomes social, it becomes moral, and the artist becomes a social moralist.

We have known him for a long time in this role. Today's predominating genre and form of literary art is the novel, and almost by nature, almost *eo ipso,* it is the social novel, social criticism. This is what it was and is everywhere, wherever it reached a flowering, in England, France, Russia, also in Italy and in the Scandinavian countries. When we come to Germany —that is another matter. What the German calls his *Innerlichkeit,* his "inwardness," renders him ill-disposed to the social and, paralleling the European social novel, Germany has produced, as we know, the more introspective genre of the educational and developmental novel. To what degree, however, even this, as a sublimation of the naive novel of adventure, is a delineation of society, is best seen in its classic example, Goethe's *Wilhelm Meister.* How easily and imperceptibly the idea of personally adventurous self-development is transformed into the educational and, as it were, against its will, flows into the social, even the political, is clearly demonstrated by this great work. Goethe had no taste for politics and was prone to count it haughtiness on the part of an artist or writer to practice criticism of social institutions. And where he did so himself, as in the wild prose scene of *Faust*—which he never cast into verse—where he pillories the cruelty of society against the fallen girl in despair that cries to heaven, he was disposed to suppress it. But to deny him social impulse, social sympathy, in fact, the deepest awareness of social destinies, that will not do. And so far as politics is concerned. . . .

So far as politics is concerned, no matter how much he warned the artist about it, even he was quite unable to solve the insoluble and to break the tie that irrevocably exists between art and politics, intellect and politics. What comes into play at this point is simply the human totality which brooks no denial. Goethe's opposition to Romanticism, to nationalistic patriotism, catholicizing whims and fancies, cult of the Middle Ages, poetic hypocrisy, and conscious obscurantism of all kinds—what else was this opposition but politics, disguised, to be sure, in aesthetic-literary garb, but basically, after all, politics of the purest breed, for the very reason that the object of his dislike, Romanticism, was itself politics, namely counter-revolution? Let people try to worm out of it by speaking of *Kulturpolitik*—cultural politics—*Geistespolitik*—intellectual politics—in false contrast with "actual" politics in the "narrower" sense. All of this only serves to confirm the indivisibility of the problem of humanity, which at no time and in no place has a "narrower sense," but includes within itself all spheres. The aesthetic, the moral, the socio-political are one within that problem of humanity.

And now, through this very unity, we become aware of a dismaying disunity: the disunited and self-contradictory quality of the intellectual spirit and of its relationship to the problem of humanity. For the human intellect is many-faceted and capable of taking *any* attiude toward the human problem, even that of inhumanity or anti-humanity. The intellect is not monolithic; it consists of no self-contained power, intent upon forming the world, life, or society after its own image. The attempt has been made, it is true, to proclaim the solidarity of all intellectuals, a completely impossible undertaking. There exists no deeper estrangement, no mutual rejection more filled with scorn and hatred, than that between the representatives of the different intellectual forms and shades of opinion. There is somehow an automatic tendency to believe that the intellect, by its very nature, takes its position, if I may use a socio-political term, on the "left," that it is therefore essentially allied with the ideas of freedom, progress, humanity. This is a prejudice which has often been disproved. The intellect can just as well take a position on the "right" and, moreover, with the greatest brilliance. Of the reactionary genius, Joseph de Maistre, the author of the work *Du Pape*, it was said by Sainte Beuve that "the only quality of a writer he possessed was talent"—a very pretty sentence, expressing that prejudiced opinion that literature and progressiveness are identical and, at the same time, admitting that it is possible for a man to be the spokesman and panegyrist—and with the greatest talent, the greatest wit and brilliance imaginable—of inhumanity, of the hangman, the stake, the inquisition, in short, of everything which liberalism and progress would call the powers of darkness.

If we take a socio-political event like the French Revolution as a criterion, what an immense gap there is between the attitude of a Michelet to this phenomenon and that of a Taine, with his only too valid critique of Jacobinism, or that of an Edmund Burke, author of *Reflections on the Revolution in France* which was translated into German by the politician of the Romantic period, Friedrich von Gentz, and exerted a monstrous influence, so far down in time that I myself in a conservative-nationalistic and anti-democratically keyed period of my own life, at the time of the first World War, quoted from this book with enthusiasm. Actually, it is a book of the first rank, and if it be a proof of the goodness of a cause that what is written in its name is *well* written, then Burke's cause was very good.

Nor let us forget that the social criticism of such an epic creator as Balzac is quite predominantly exercised from the "right," just as, after all, a product of bourgeois-capitalistic society like Baron de Nucingen can be criticized just as well from the right as from the left. In our own days we have a fascinating case of conservative or, if you will, reactionary, social criticism, placed in the most refined and artistically advanced setting, in the person of the late Knut Hamsun—an apostate of liberalism, formatively influenced by Dostoievski and Nietzsche, filled with hatred for civilization, for city life, industrialism, intellectualism and all that sort of thing, above all passionately anti-English and so pro-German that, when Hitler arrived, he subscribed to National Socialism with active enthusiasm and became a traitor to his country. No one who really knew his work—the work of a great writer—could have been surprised at this intellectual course and personal destiny. One needed only to remember how amusingly, with what mordant wit, he had derided certain historical typifications of liberalism, such as Victor Hugo and Gladstone, in his earliest books. But what was an interesting intellectual attitude, what was paradox and *belles lettres* in 1895, became acute politics in 1933 and seriously and painfully darkened a world-wide literary reputation.

Closely related to the Hamsun phenomenon is the case of Ezra Pound, another stirring example of the deep cleavage of the intellect in its relationship to the problem of society. A bold artist and literary avant-gardist, he threw himself into the arms of Fascism, made propaganda for it during the second World War as a political activist, and lost the game through the military victory of Democracy, this victory which has since become such a problem to Democracy itself. After he had been judged guilty and confined as a traitor, a jury of distinguished Anglo-American writers awarded him a very highly esteemed literary distinction, the Bollingen Prize—and thereby manifested a high degree of independence of the aesthetic judgment from politics. Or was politics after all not as far removed from this judgment as it appeared to be? I am surely not the only one who would like to know whether the distinguished jury would have awarded the Bollingen Prize to Ezra Pound if, by chance, he had not been a Fascist but a Communist.

A mere remark like this one doubtless suffices today to place the man who utters it under the suspicion of Communism. This suspicion would do me an injustice or, if you like, do me too much honor. I am very badly equipped to provide an example of the Communist; my works are surely filled with all the vices abhorred and abominated by Communism, such as formalism, psychologism, skepticism, decadent tendencies and what-have-you; not to forget humor and a certain weakness for the truth—for love of the truth is weakness in the eyes of strict partisanship. And yet one must make a distinction here. Communism is an idea, an idea which is badly distorted in its reality, but whose roots reach deeper than Marxism and Stalinism and whose pure realization will again and again confront mankind as a challenge and a task. Fascism is not an idea at all but a wickedness to which, let us hope, no people, small or great, will ever again surrender itself. Fascism it was which, through its victories and its not wholly desired defeat, drove me more and more to the left in social philosophy and, at times, actually made me into a kind of itinerant orator for Democracy, a role whose comic qualities, even at the time of my most passionate longing for Hitler's downfall, were never hidden from my view.

Undeniably, the political moralizing of an artist has something comic about it, and propaganda for humanitarian ideals brings him almost inevitably into proximity—and not only into proximity—with the platitude. This I have learned; and if I just now assigned the socially reactionary tendencies of an author to the realm of paradox, so to speak as a contradiction between his vocation and his way of practicing it, I was nevertheless very well aware that this paradox and this contradiction may possess a high degree of intellectual charm, that they are intellectually more rewarding and afford an incomparably better protection from banality than being politically good-natured does. It is very much a question, or rather it is scarcely any question, who was the intellectually more interesting political writer, Joseph de Maistre or Victor Hugo. But if there is no question of this, then another question steps in its place, whether, in political matters, in contact with human wants and needs, it is so much a question of being interesting rather than of being good.

"Almost too good to be true" is the way an English critic, Philip Toynbee, has characterized the political attitude which I have taken for the past thirty years. I refer to an article by him in the *Observer* called "The Isolated World Citizen," a mere seven hundred words, the most correct thing which has been said about my existence by anyone in England and perhaps anywhere else. Young Toynbee is right: there is something slightly questionable about this attitude, about everything in it that smacks of optimism, democratism, humanitarianism, faith in humanity—and even about my "world citizenship." For my books are desperately German, and whatever intrusion into socio-political questions occurs in them was not only gained at the cost of natural modesty but also wrung from the pessimism of a mind that had gone through Schopenhauer's school and is basically inept at a generously humanitarian gesture. Out with it: I do not have much faith, nor do I believe very much in faith, but far more in a goodness capable of existing without faith and which can even be the direct product of doubt.

Lessing said of his drama, *Nathan the Wise:* "It is certainly not a satiric piece, to leave the arena with scornful laughter. It is to be as moving a piece of work as I have ever achieved." Instead of "satiric" he could have said "nihilistic" if the word had already been available to him, and instead of "moving" he could have said "kind" in order to protest against the preconceived idea that, because he was a doubter, he was promoting despair. Art, no matter how bitter an accusation it may bring, no matter how deeply it may bemoan the corruption of creation, regardless of how far it may go in its ironic treatment of reality and even of itself—it does not lie within its nature to "leave the arena with scornful laughter." It does not shake the cold diabolical fist of nihilism in the face of life, for whose spiritual animation it was made. It is allied with the good and its foundation is goodness, closely akin to wisdom, even more closely to love. If it likes to make mankind laugh, it is still not scornful laughter that it offers but a gladness in which hate and stupidity are dissolved, a serenity that frees and unites. Born anew again and again from solitude, its effect is to unite. It is the last to harbor any illusions about its influence upon human destiny. Despiser of all that is bad, it has never yet been able to arrest the victory of evil; intent upon meaning, it has never been able to prevent the most incredible madness. It is not a power, it is only a consolation. And yet, a game of the deepest seriousness, the paradigm of all striving toward perfection, it was given to mankind from the very beginning as a companion, and from its innocence mankind will never be able to turn its guilt-saddened eye utterly away.

Theatre and Literature

LUIGI PIRANDELLO

Dramatic authors, *professionals of the theatre*, disdain to be considered literary men, because they say and insist that the theatre is theatre and not literature.

We do not wish to be so malicious as to believe that this disdain is based largely on the *serious* amount of their earnings when compared with the ridiculous *jest* of the paltry income of the poor deluded ones who are the pure literati.

Certainly for their part, they have managed the business of the theatre like any kind of commercial institution, which defends itself from other commercial institutions interested in sharing the same business: the star performers and the owners and the managers of the theatres. They have established the procedure for giving their productions to this or that company; for the assignment of "places"; for a percentage of the receipts fixed in advance, so much for the first performance, so much for the second, so much for the subsequent ones, collection of which is in the hands of the Society of Authors of Milan, which at the end of every three months sends to the members an accounting of the proceeds, which to speak truly—however badly a drama or comedy goes—always greatly exceeds that of any other writer, whether of short stories or novels (for Heaven's sake let us not speak of poets!), from the sale of his books.

There is no doubt that all this has nothing to do with literature. We can also grant, as they themselves prefer, that truly *their* theatre, that is, their more or less abundant production of dramas or comedies shipped to the theatrical market, is not litera-

"Teatro e Letteratura" appeared in the newspaper, *Il Messaggero della Domenica*, July 30, 1918. Translated by A. M. Webb.

ture. It remains to be seen, however, as it is not literature, how and under what new species their dramas and comedies must be considered when from acting copies they become books, when from the prompter's box they pass to the show windows of a book seller, no longer typewritten but printed by a publisher, when, after the lavish income that the voice and gesture of the actors have drawn from the boards of the stage, they descend to beg meanly for three lire, the price of the cover, among those other beggars exposed to public charity that are the volumes of stories and novels of the indigent pure literati.

But once and for all, let us drop this accounting and consider our own situation. Here there is a great misunderstanding to clear up, which consists precisely in the word *literature*.

Dramatic authors, professionals of the theatre, write badly, not only because they do not know how to write well and never tried to do so, but because they believe conscientiously that writing well for the theatre is for literary men, and they claim that they have to write in that somewhat conversational style which those who know nothing of literature employ, because the characters of their dramas and comedies—they say—not being literary people, cannot talk on the stage as such. That is clear; they must speak the way every one speaks. No literature.

Saying all this, they have not the remotest idea that they confuse *good* writing with *fine* writing, or rather, they do not see that they fall into this error: that *good* writing means *fine* writing; and they do not think that the fine writing of certain would-be men of letters, viewed from an aesthetic standpoint, presents the same vice from the other extreme as their bad writing: literature which is not art means bad literature, whether it is *fine* writing or whether it is *bad* writing, and as such it must be condemned, even though those who write in this way do not wish to pass for literary men.

To write a drama or comedy well does not mean to make the characters speak in a literary form, that is, in a language not spoken and in itself literary. This is *fine* writing. They must be made to speak as they *ought* to speak, given their character, their situation, and circumstances in the various moments of the action. And this does not mean at all that the language must be common or unliterary. What does "unliterary" mean if one seeks to make a work of art? The language will never be *common* because it will be *appropriate* to a given personage in a given scene, *appropriate* to his character, his passion, or his action. And if the characters all speak in their own way, and not with the vulgar clumsiness of an inexact approximate language which merely denotes the author's incapacity to find the exact expression because he does not know how to write, the comedy will be well written; and a comedy that is written well, if it is also well conceived and well developed, is a literary work of art in the same way as a good novel or a good story or a fine lyric poem.

The truth is that dramatic authors, professionals of the theatre, have all remained fixed to that blessed poetics of naturalism, which confused physical, mental, and aesthetic creations in so gracious a way, that to aesthetic creation it came to give (at least theoretically, because in practice it was impossible to do so) that character of mechanical necessity and fixity which belongs to the physical fact.

Now, we must bear in mind that art, whatever its form (let us say literary art, of which the dramatic is but one of many forms), is not imitation and reproduction, but *creation*. The question of language, if it is as it ought to be spoken; the pretended difficulty of finding in Italy a language truly spoken throughout the whole nation, and the other question of a truly Italian national life that is lacking in order to give substance and character to a theatre which can be called Italian, precisely as if the nature and function of art were the necessary reproduction of this life, which each one can recognize through external data and facts; and all the other distressing nonsense and vain superstition of the so-called technique which should mirror (only in theory, of course, because in practice it is not possible) action as we see it take place before our eyes in everyday reality —all this is the willful torment of the voluntary martyrs of an absurd system, of a poetic aberration, fortunately in large part long since overcome, but to which, I repeat, the professionals of the theatre show that they remain bound.

It is not a question of imitating or of reproducing life; for the very simple reason that there is no life which constitutes a reality in itself, to be reproduced, with its own characteristics. Life is a continual and indistinct flowing and has no other form outside of that which we give it from time to time, infinitely varied and constantly changing. Each one in reality creates for himself his own life; this creation, however, is never free, not only because it is subject to all of the natural and social necessities which limit things, men, and their actions, and deform and contradict them to the point of making them fail and fail miserably; it is never free, too, because in the creation of our life our will moves almost always, not to say absolutely always, toward aims of practical utility, to arrive at a position in society, and the like, that lead to selfish actions and impose renunciations or duties that are naturally limitations of liberty.

Only art, when it is true art, creates freely: creates, that is, a reality which has its necessity, its laws, its aims, only in itself, because the will no longer acts outwardly, conquering all the obstacles which are opposed to those ends of practical utility toward which we move in that other, selfish creation, I mean in that which all of us try to create, every day of our life, to the extent that we can; but the will acts inwardly in the life to which we seek to give form, and precisely out of this form, still within us, but already alive for itself and hence as it were entirely independent of us, it becomes movement. And this is the true and the only technique: the will thought of as free, spontaneous, and immediate movement of form; I mean, when we are no longer ourselves willing this form thus and so, for an end of our own; but when it is absolutely free, because it has no other end except in itself, it which wills, it which produces in itself and in us the acts capable of making it into a body: statue, picture, book; and only then is the aesthetic act completed.

Outside of us, usually, the actions that bring a character into relief intersect on a background of valueless contingencies, of particulars common to all. Vulgar, unforeseen, and unexpected obstacles turn aside actions, debase characters; little accidental misfortunes often reduce them. Art frees things, men, and their actions from these valueless contingencies, from these common particulars, from these vulgar obstacles, from these accidental misfortunes. In a certain sense, it abstracts them; that is, rejects, without noticing it, all that interferes with the artist's conception, and on the other hand, brings together all that is in harmony with it, gives it greater strength and richness. It thus creates a work which is not, like nature, without order (at least apparently so) and bristling with contradictions, but something like a little world in which all the elements hold together in turn and move together in turn. Precisely in this sense the artist idealizes. Not indeed that he represents types or depicts ideas: he simplifies and concentrates. The idea he has of his characters, the feeling that rises from them, evoke the expressive images, group and combine them. Useless details disappear; all that is inherent in the living logic of the characters is reunited, concentrated in the unity of a being that is, let us say, less real and yet more true.

But see now in what consists the unerring suggestion of the theatre with respect to a work of art which has already had its definitive, unique expression in the writer's pages. That which is already expression, that which is already form must become substance; a substance to which the actors, according to their means and their capacity, must in turn give form. Since the actor, if he does not wish (nor can he wish) that the written words of the drama come from his mouth as from a megaphone or from a phonograph, must indeed reconceive the character, he reconceives it in his way for his own part. The image already expressed must return to organize itself in him and tends to become the movement that brings it about and makes it real on the stage. For him, too, in sum, the execution must spring alive from the conception, and only by virtue of it, by movements thus set in motion by the image itself, alive and active, existing not only inside of him but having become soul and body with him and in him.

Now even though it is not born spontaneously in the actor, but is aroused in his mind by the expression of the writer, can this image ever be the same? Can it ever be unaltered, unchanged, in passing from one mind to another? It will no longer be the same. It will indeed be an approximate image, more or less like it; but the same, no. A given character on the stage will speak the same words as are in the written drama, but the character will never be that of the poet, because the actor has recreated him in himself, and the expression is the actor's although the words are not; the voice, the body, the gesture, all are his.

The literary work is the drama and the comedy conceived and written by the poet; what will be seen in the theatre is not and cannot be anything but a scenic translation. So many actors, so many translations, more or less faithful, more or less fortunate, but like any translation, always and necessarily inferior to the original.

For if we think about it, the actor must do and does of necessity the opposite of what the poet has done. He renders the character created by the poet more real and yet less true; that is, he takes from him as much of that ideal, superior truth as he gives back to him of that material, common reality; and he makes him less true too because he translates him into the conventional and fictitious reality of a stage. The actor, in sum, necessarily gives an artificial consistency in a false and illusory environment to persons and actions who have already had an expression of ideal life, which is that of art, and who live and breathe in a higher reality.

Well, then? Are dramatic authors right who see nothing but the theatre and who say and insist that the theatre is theatre and not literature?

If by theatre we mean that place where evening and daily performances occur, with actors to whom they give the subject and material to make up, almost on the spot, striking dramatic and comic scenes, yes. But in that case, as far as art is concerned, one must be willing to share the same position as those easy versifiers who compose little poems for certain illustrated reviews.

They write not for the text but for the translation. And truly, their theatre has no use for literature. Nothing but material for actors, to which actors will give life and consistency on the stage; in fact, something like the scenario of the *commedia dell'arte*.

But for us the theatre must be something else.

The New Theatre and the Old

LUIGI PIRANDELLO

You may be familiar with the anecdote of the poor peasant who, when he heard his parish priest say that he could not read because he had left his glasses at home, spurred his wit and conceived the fancy idea that knowing how to read depended upon having a pair of eyeglasses. Consequently, he journeyed to the city and went to an optometrist's shop and demanded "Glasses for reading."

But since no pair of glasses succeeded in making the poor man read, the optometrist, at the end of his patience, after having turned his shop upside down, snarled, "But, tell me, can you read?" Amazed at this, the peasant answered, "That's a good one, and if I knew how to read, why would I have come to you?"

Well, now, all those who have neither a thought or feeling of their own to express, and think that to compose a comedy, a drama, or even a tragedy it is enough to write an imitation of someone else, should have the courage and the frankness of naive wonder of this poor peasant.

To the question, "But really, have you something of your own to tell us?" they should have the courage and the frankness to answer, "That's a good one! And if we had something of our own to say, would we write like someone else?"

But I realize that this might really be asking too much.

"Teatro nuovo e teatro vecchio" is the text of a lecture by Luigi Pirandello delivered in Venice in July, 1922, and published in *Comoedia*, January 1, 1923. In May, 1934, Pirandello presented the lecture, with modifications, at Turin. This revised text first appeared in *La Stampa* (Turin) May 13, 1934, and is reprinted in Pirandello's *Saggi* (edited by Manlio Lo Vecchio Musti), Arnoldo Mondadori, Milan, 1952, pp. 250-267. Translated by Herbert Goldstone.

Maybe it would be enough that all these persons should not become so angry when somebody calmly points out that while it is true that no one forbids them the exercise of writing and rewriting a theatre already written, doing this means that they do not have eyes of their own but a pair of borrowed glasses.

It has been said and repeated that, in general, the imitative or decorative faculty in the nature of the Latin character is superior to the creative or inventive, and that the whole history of our theatre, and in general of our literature, is fundamentally nothing but a perpetual repetition of imitated manners; and that, looking at our literary history, we certainly find very many glasses, and very few eyes, and that our writers did not disdain glasses but were proud to use ancient lenses to see in the manner of Plautus or Terence or Seneca, who in their turn had seen in the manner of the Greek tragedies, Menander, and of middle Athenian comedy. But these—shall we say—visual aids were at least made at home from rhetoric which always came from our own optometrist shop; and these glasses passed from one nose to another, through generations and generations of noses, until suddenly, with the rise of Romanticism, the cry was raised, "Gentlemen, let us try to look with our own eyes." They tried; but, alas, they were able to see very little. And the importation of foreign glasses began.

An old story. And I should not have mentioned it if, truly, things had not everywhere reached such a state that to obtain public favor it is not so necessary to have a pair of one's own eyes, as to have a pair of someone else's eyeglasses, which make you see men and life in a certain manner and with a given color, that is, as fashion urges or current public taste commands. And woe to whoever disdains or refuses to put them on his nose, or who is obstinate enough to want to look at men and life in his own way; his vision, if simple, will be called bare; if sincere, vulgar; if intimate and acute, obscure and paradoxical; and the natural expression of this new world will always appear filled with the greatest defects.

I will speak again of these defects. The greatest and best known has been in every age that of "writing badly." It is distressing to acknowledge it, but all the original visions of life are always badly expressed. At least they were always so judged at their first appearance, especially by that plague of society, the so-called cultivated and nice people.

Recently I have much enjoyed reading a piece of Clive Bell attacking these same people. Here and there, he says, a man of powerful intellect is able to succeed in forcing the gates; but cultivated people do not like originality, not as long as it looks original. The company of the man of original talent is not pleasant, at least not until he is dead. Cultivated people adore whoever gives them, in some unsuspected way, just what they have learned to expect, and, fundamentally, they do not like art any more than do the Philistines; except that they want to have the sensation of seeing the old cloaked in the new; and, for that reason, they prefer those pastry cooks who sprinkle a little art on their common thoughts and feelings. Because of this, culture (so understood) is even more dangerous than Philistinism: it pretends to be on the side of the artist; it has the "charm" of its exquisite taste, yet it can corrupt because it can speak with an authority denied the Philistines; and because it feigns an interest in art, often the artists are not indifferent to its judgments. It is necessary, therefore, to free the artist and also the public from the influence of the opinion of the cultivated. And the liberation will not be complete until those who have already learned to scorn the opinion of the petty bourgeoisie will also learn to ignore the disapproval of people constrained by their limited power of feeling to consider art an elegant entertainment.

Gentlemen, for the cultivated fifteenth century Dante wrote badly; *The Divine Comedy* was badly written, and not only because it was not composed in Latin, but in the language of the people and really badly written in that same popular idiom. And Machiavelli? He writes *The Prince* and shamefully has to excuse himself and confess that he was not cultivated enough to write it better. And to the fanatic admirers of the flowery Tasso did not also Ariosto's *Orlando Furioso* seem badly written? And Vico's *New Science* appeared not only badly but terribly written; he had the curious fate of starting to write in a completely different manner, so as to seem somebody else when he decided to please all those who were accustomed to read with the glasses of that rhetoric which he later habitually professed.

To conclude this discussion of eyes and eyeglasses, the joke, nevertheless, is that all who wear the glasses (and all cultivated people wear them, or at least one supposes that they must have them, and the more so as they may pretend not to be aware of it), preach that in art it is absolutely necessary to have one's own eyes; yet at the same time they criticize any one who uses them, whether well or badly, because, let us make it clear, while these people say writers should use their own eyes, they must be and see exactly as the cultivated people's eyes, which, however, are only glasses, for if they fall and break, then it is good night.

Ever since foreign importation began in the theatre world, these eyeglasses have been bought—it is too obvious to point out— in Paris, a market which has become international only for such wares. In fact, the most renowned French factories are now on the decline, and not a few have lost all credit. The illusory eyeglasses of the Sardou firm were once greatly used almost everywhere. Someone, and not without profit and consideration, still continues using them among us, incredible as it may seem. But nothing is often more incredible than the truth. A pair of lenses for the near-sighted, very powerful, and strongly recommended for acute and precise clarity, were those of the firm of Becque with the trademark of "Parisian." And another pair, justly valued for a certain idealizing virtue, were those of the house of de Curel. But there came from far-off Norway, first on the German market and then on the French, the powerful glasses of Henrik Ibsen, to impose themselves through a very different investigating power of ideal and social values. The vogue lasted a long time, though few succeeded in adjusting these eyeglasses to their noses; then, after they recognized this difficulty as almost insurmountable, there came into fashion the monocles of the firm of Bataille and Bernstein, which sold widely in all the countries of the world. And, finally, and alas, without the least fault nor the slightest pleasure of the inventor, there is a certain Pirandello lens, called a diabolical brand by the malicious, which makes you see double and triple and slanted, and in short, makes you see the world upside down. Many still use these lenses, despite the fact that I do not miss any occasion to make them know that such lenses ruin their eyesight. On the one hand for support, and on the other for the good digestion of the honest citizen, a pair of lenses can be found today, lenses at a good price and easily used, for colored diversion and natural comfort, and in two colors: a comic eye and a sentimental eye. Every barber with the slightest dramatic aspiration is able to supply them, confident of quickly acquiring a fine reputation and of making a hatful of money.

But I must speak to you of the new theatre and the old, and I have spoken to you until now of eyes and eyeglasses: that is, of original creation and the exercise of imitation. This carries its own explanation. I do not want to criticize even this copying exercise which was and always will be typical of all the old theatre. I do not criticize it—do you know why?—even to irritate the devotees of that other vice of civil society, that is, "pure" literary criticism. To them, every debate on the theatre appears almost unworthy of their attention and consideration, unless as a pardonable exception it is used as an expressive form by some poet who is otherwise important and respected. And even then, if this "pure" literary criticism talks about theatre, naturally it avoids wasting a word or casting a glance, even in passing, at all that stage armament which sustains the habitual conception of a theatre, "played," as they say, according to its well-defined "rules," and spoken in its well-defined gibberish and regulated scene by scene with means and effects of its own stage. Everyone agrees that a work of the theatre should be understood as neither more nor less than a work of art; and that only on this condition is it worth discussing. Very well. But let us reflect a little. To refuse all literary expression to the products of such a trade by being hermetically silent about it—as one does when the monopoly is controlled by those writers of comedies who are proud to declare themselves of a "trade" acquired through assiduous training on the stage, and who feel they must defend the stage as their small, exclusive, inviolable domain protected all around by so many posters stating "entrance prohibited to outsiders"—may be right, without doubt, in so many ways; but, excuse me if I should point out to you that nevertheless out of that profession, when a sudden inspiration invests and ennobles it, although leaving it for the most part a trade, so many beautiful and great comedies have come. What then?

Even in England in Shakespeare's time, even in Spain at the time of Lope de Vega and Calderón de la Barca, or even in France at the time of Molière, the theatre was a trade reserved to the "specialist," to those who knew the stage, and they remade fifty times the same plots, filled with the same spirit common to a whole generation, and the priority of the ideas did not matter at all and the personality of the writer very little, and the greater part of the comedies, written in twenty-four hours, served as a spectacle for an evening and then was discarded among the rummage. There was no artistic seriousness, in the sense of high literary criticism and of cultivated and nice people. But *La vida es sueño*, to cite only one example, was still forged at that smithy. And what then?

It then appears clear to me that in the field of art every polemic, every critical attitude, every theory, if postulated and developed systematically and abstractly, *a priori* or *a posteriori*, whether discussed according to intellectual or moral criteria, or even from a purely aesthetic point of view, risks continually being disarranged and turned topsy turvy or remaining bewildered at the disconcerting appearance of the created work, which is without original sin and finds citizenship and status in the kingdom of art from wherever it comes; the crux is that it got there.

Until now, we have anticipated a brief preface on original creation and imitative exercise (eyes and eyeglasses) apropos of the new theatre and the old; and a negative judgment on the polemics of art stated and developed systematically and abstractly. If you let me pause a little on this point, I will give you reasons for both prefaces.

Let us ask: is it possible or not to recognize in the work of the theatre a value of art, of achieved expression, from the assumption of its "newness," understanding by newness a harmony between the content and the particular spirit of revision and reconstruction of intellectual values which animates our times in every field: politics, science, philosophy, art itself? Are not the comedies or dramas in harmony with this spirit new theatre, that is, in this sieve, grain from which we can extract the best of the living work of art—while those comedies and those dramas which do not absorb this new spirit remain chaff, without any hope of salvation? Let us examine this a little. Is it possible, then, that criticism may direct with a certain sureness the activity of writers, instead of following it and explaining it, and that it may direct it with maximum profit for all, and especially of the young still in search of an expression of their own, toward particular problems, without which there is no hope of constructing new and vital works? If this were so, we should without ado immediately ask literary criticism to set forth such problems. But probably criticism would answer that to enunciate them, or to define them, is as good as to resolve them and, therefore, to destroy them as problems; and that this is the task of authors and not of critics.

Every one sees that in this way the question is badly put; and that, so put, it cannot be resolved. To resolve it, as a work of art, we must look fully into the fundamental problems of form and the aesthetic fact; and we will then see clearly that the "new" in art is nothing more than one of the many necessary values of every created work. We need not discuss in abstraction, stating and denying as exterior and existent for themselves, certain indeterminate problems from which we determine the "new." The open minds, the creative spirits find them indeed, but without searching for them—here is the essential point—and attack them, but without perhaps even knowing them in their abstract terms, and, without study, resolve them. Because it is not true that these problems are of a particular time, or that creative spirits can assume them from time.

If these minds are truly creative, the problems belong to the minds themselves and are not an indistinctive and indeterminate fact in time; but indistinct and undetermined points of the active spirit itself, which just because he has them himself as a part of his nature, as a living effort, can find the strength to free himself from them by expressing them. And they are active problems just because they are not enunciated by criticism but are expressed through the means of art. That is to say, they are not defined by the pure intellect which chills and solidifies them, and naturally kills them, as problems, merely by enunciating them; but they have to be represented through the means of art in a form which is the construction and the *raison d'être* of their eternal life.

What is our time outside of the meaning and value that we give it? I say, we, with our spirit.

Now, think! Who can give meaning and value to his time, not a particular meaning and value functioning in the moments of the life of a single individual, but universal, in which each person can always find himself, if not the man who can speak with the most absolute disinterestedness, so that his voice can sound as his own in the breast of whoever listens? Not the person who satisfies material ambitions for himself in life, but the one who affirms "my kingdom is not of this world" and nevertheless affirms that he has a kingdom; who, therefore, creates life for himself and for all; who, therefore, succeeds in making consistent his own organic and total vision of life; who, therefore, is like the whole and pure spirit which is able to reveal itself fully; he is the poet, the maker, the creator: he will be able to give to his time a universal meaning and value because with his own absolute disinterestedness he makes all the concerns of his frank and lively senses (his own new eyes), thoughts and relationships of concepts, feelings, images assume in him an autonomous and complete organic unity, and he wants to realize that unity in himself which life freely wants for itself, so that he, in this sense, is a spirit servant of the spirit, the creator servant of his creation. In the organic wholeness of life he has a place like all the others; he has created not to dominate and rule, but to systematize. And for that reason, Christ, poet, maker, creator of reality, called himself son of man and gave meaning and value to life for all men.

The problems of time, therefore, do not exist for him who creates.

They exist for those men, undoubtedly worthy of the greatest respect because they are enlightened and enlighten others, but who do not have truly creative qualities in their spirit; these people take them truly from time, where the creative spirits have placed them.

In fact, every creation, every vision of life, every revelation of the spirit, necessarily carries within itself problems, questions, logical contradictions, the more decisive and evident as these creations, visions, and revelations are organic and comprehensive: and this simply because mystery is congenital to the spirit, and to look with new eyes, to express frankly, to reorganize life is to project life once more in mystery. To make: to create, anew, from nothing: that nothing is felt again necessarily by all with greater strength. Little by little, however, the anxiety of every first intuition will be appeased, as well as the dismay or also the annoyance which humanity always experiences in looking again at these objects: fortunately, our nature is such that it is allowed to sleep. But at first an almost general elevation of the spirit makes reborn those problems, those questions, the warning of those contradictions which have always been the same, but which now reappear as new because they have a new value. It is almost impossible that the new sense of life may be hit upon directly from the beginning. The problems appear obscure, and the spirit which agitates them, paradoxical. The so-called "logic," unmasked, has been driven out of life.

The sense of revelation is obscure if we blame its expression, especially when we deal with a work of art. The case is different if it is a question of a religious revelation or a new philosophical revelation.

Because if we treat of a revelation in which faith enters as a necessary and essential element, the problems that revelation brings with it are naturally set aright if we accept faith; or, otherwise, they immediately lose any consistency and, for that reason, any stimulus and power to create doubt, to make intellectual systems waver, and finally, to be discussed passionately.

And if we treat of problems set forth in new intellectual constructions of philosophy, through the same technical and conventional language in which they are stated, they already appear connected to certain currents of thought already expressed, and the troublesome sense of the "new," which they are able to awaken is, for that reason, always somewhat limited and relative; but they are immediately evaluated perfectly, in their precise terms, and this annuls every spiritual restlessness over whatever may appear indistinct, imprecise, and ambiguous in its expressions. Every mind which becomes conscious of them has in so doing immediately tested them in all their parts. Furthermore, by their conceptual nature, that is, abstracted from life, in the light of criticism they can be displaced, completed, annulled, or resolved.

But not the problems represented in a new work of art. They remain and always will remain as they have been fixed: problems of life. Their irreducibility consists in their expression as representation. Think of Hamlet: to be or not to be. Take this problem from Hamlet's mouth, empty it of Hamlet's passion, conceptualize it in philosophical terms, and in the light of criticism you may play with it as long as you like. But leave it there on Hamlet's lips a living expression, an active representation of the torment of that life, and the problem of being or not being will never be resolved in eternity. And not only for Hamlet, a single spirit in a definite moment of his life, but for every spirit who contemplates that form of life, and—for this is Art—lives it. And these problems are in that form, and will always be, for every one, problems of life. Thus, they live through the form, through the expression.

They are able to live in this way because their expression is finished, completed.

The perfect form has detached them entirely, both alive and concrete; that is, fluid and indistinct from time and from space, and has fixed them forever, has gathered them into itself, that which is incorruptible, as if embalming them alive.

At so great a distance of time, humanity without still having resolved them, has adjusted itself to them. It has succeeded in putting itself in that state of aesthetic contemplation in which it calls them beautiful, still feeling them as problems of life.

With the meaning and value they have assumed, organized in that way, humanity can now contemplate them without any anguish. It knows, and by now is accustomed to know that, in that vision of life, mystery appears in this way. For it is not the sense of mystery which terrifies men, since they know that mystery is in life; the unusual way of representing something new is what terrifies. Now that way is no longer new. But has it for that reason become old? No. How can it become old, if it is represented in action, in perfect, incorruptible form? Only the time has come in which we have discovered it "created," in which all the reasons of its being are seen to consist in the necessity of its being what it is; and no longer new, never old, not arbitrary, or obscure, or imprecise, or unfinished, but finally necessary in every way: *that*, and that alone which it had to be.

But it might be instructive to read once more about the anger stirred up in the heart of Voltaire, for example, even at a distance of two centuries. And an almost contemporary critic of Michelangelo, in a solemn attack, harshly criticizes him for having made an arbitrary and absolutely illogical work, depicting in the "Pietà" the Virgin as a girl scarcely eighteen who holds on her knee the thirty-three year old Son. Now we understand what depth of poetry Michelangelo reached in the representation of that Madonna, the Virgin, who conceived through grace and is always the girl of the "Annunciation," compared to the Son, the Redeemer, who has had to bear all the pain of the world. But how that same critic boasted of having opened Michelangelo's eyes and of inviting him to correct properly his inconceivable aberration! As if one might wish to enlighten Hamlet's mind in order to help him resolve in some way the confusion of his problems.

Now we would laugh and no longer think of this; but because

it is a matter of Hamlet and of Michelangelo's "Pietà"—artistic expressions for which we have finally found the *ubi consistam* of aesthetic evaluation which explains the being of their life: the necessity which the form represents.

Still, because contemporary criticism does not give enough weight to the absolute difference between the philosophical problem set forth through concepts in an intellectual construction and the problem of life expressed in the immediate representation of art—creator of form, in this sense inviolable—very often today this criticism of contemporary works of art avoids probing as deeply as it could, not merely into the representation of a spiritual debate accidentally expressed in the work, but into the very objects of that debate, and tries instead to discover its logical contradictions and looks only at the conceptual design of the work of art. This has happened to me and to my work. But the conceptual framework, on the one hand, is absolutely nothing more than a pretext, a stimulus to create, and, therefore, in the evaluation of the created work (which is considered in itself and by itself) could not and must not find a place. On the other hand, the conceptual framework is at best no more than a scheme, a skeleton, which becomes immediately incorporated, wholly reabsorbed, in the whole of the expressive elaboration of the work, and not even from this side, therefore, can it lead to a just aesthetic evaluation. And just as bad, it seems to me, is criticism generally done by those who still would like to do it according to its correct principles, based, I mean, upon expression. Especially when these people come upon new material expressed for the first time.

We have declared what seemed to us the reasons for which this first expression must at the beginning appear muddled, obscure, arbitrary, paradoxical: a "badly written" work. These difficult judges, among other things, do not consider that the very fury with which they penetrate into the limits of the problems represented in the work of art in order to combat them and destroy them, and define them in themselves, this very fury from which they then resolve the judgment that the work of art is not completely expressed, is, instead, the surest and clearest testimony

that the incriminated expression is still that which it had to be:
so that they have been able to draw out and fight these problems
face to face as alive and present, and which are therefore represented, and perfectly so, in an achieved form.

But it is natural that conflict and misunderstanding exist for
those who have eyes and create, and not for those who have
glasses and copy in a final draft the obscure, abstruse expressions
of creators who "write badly" and diligently clean up all those
"errors," so that one fine day when a taste will have developed
for the new expression, these qualities will reveal themselves as
their necessary "traits."

Think that even Goldoni, who today seems as simple and
accessible as it is possible to imagine, whose style seems so pure
and faithful to the reality of his characters lifted bodily from the
pressure of the life of his time; even Goldoni was not recognized
in his own time. And how they criticized him! They said that he
wrote badly, and they all said it to him, right away, even those
who with due reservations accepted his theatre and followed him.
They seemed to say to him, "Yes you are right; those who criticize you understand nothing, but if only you knew how to write
a little better!"

And this is natural, if we think that the spirit always brings to
life its creations with great and slow labor and that every time it
succeeds in establishing one of them it experiences the need of
resting for a while. In this way, therefore, certain periods come
after the recognition of every original expression, certain periods
in which spirits no longer truly create but devote themselves to
small discoveries of illuminating the details of the vision of life
which is present at that moment, so that all remains impregnated
in it; and we have established, besides, a heavy burden of clichés
which have meaning for all in that moment and perhaps have
none after the advent of a new original expression; we have
established, I was saying, a world absolutely determined, perhaps
more by expression than by conception, which is not really the
same for all, naturally, but which is stamped with the same char-

acteristics. Take the writings of men of a certain time, anonymous in the sense that they are called neither Shakespeare nor Dante, and you can recognize, without looking at the date, those written by our fathers, grandfathers, and ancestors. There are some who write with great clarity of expression, with grace, with a beautiful periodic style. There! These men write well. And why does Carlo Goldoni write badly? Because his expressions, in order to define a new vision of life, necessarily had to be different from those that were in the ears of all, already composed, already studied and for that reason very clear, and which anyone, by Jove, with a bit of talent and good will, could embellish gracefully. And that clumsy Goldoni. . . .

I believe that every creator, besides his great sins, ought to feel on his conscience the secret afflictions of his contemporary admirers, almost as a sense of shame because of his inevitable bad writing. And Goldoni should have more remorse than any one. The dialogue of Carlo Goldoni must have appeared, even to his admirers, insipid and specious, compared to the language of the *commedia dell'arte*; and badly written, legalistic, and formless enough to make you sick compared to the style of the serious compositions of the time.

The *commedia dell'arte* which was, indeed, played spontaneously, but which was incapable of imposing itself as a true improvisation, was at bottom only the quintessence of the commonplace, based on generic themes and ready-made patterns contrived to frame the same repertory of stereotyped phrases, typical, and traditional jokes and epigrams, and ritualized blows and retorts, phrased as though in a manual of etiquette. It was natural for everyone that on the stage it should be so spoken: since a taste had been developed for conventions which ruled that language, one went to the theatre to admire the undisguised witticisms, the false naturalness, and false spontaneity; and the style of Goldoni had to appear fallacious because it was psychological, insipid because it was natural, and it undid with its dialogue the fixity of those lines and loosened the rigidity of the masks, cutting apart little by little their consistency and expressing it—a new and unknown spectacle—through the free play of all the liberated muscles.

But why couldn't Goldoni, who still experienced in life the struggling fate of the innovator, fix himself as an absolute value, so that he could face those who have made almost a fetish of him and who, with the intention of praising him, exclaim, "Oh, the good 'old' Goldoni!" (and that "old" expresses, more than a real intrinsic recognition, a spirit of polemic with "new") and altogether deny him any value in himself and regard his production as an outdated moment in the history of the Italian theatre, and deny that it can be the expression of a created and insurmountable world in the eternal kingdom of art?

This too—I think—comes about through the ambiguities to which the abstract and systematic evaluations are subject.

It is natural that each finished work—a created world unique in itself, and beyond comparison, which no longer can be new or old but simply "that which it is" in itself and for itself eternally, finds in its very "uniqueness" the reasons, first, of its incomprehension, and then, always, of its frightening solitude: the solitude of things which have been expressed in this way, immediately, as they wanted to be, and, therefore, "for themselves alone." And because of this single fact alone they would be impossible to know, if each person wanting to know them did not make them escape from that being "for themselves alone," making them exist for him, as he interprets and understands them.

Who knows Dante as he was for himself in his poem! Dante in his existence for himself becomes like nature: we should have to go out of ourselves to understand him as he is for himself, and we can not, and each one understands him as he can in his own way. Dante remains truly alone in his divine solitude. Nevertheless, each age makes him its own; each age echoes in its own way his unique voice.

But actually, the voice of Dante speaks eternal things; he speaks from the very insides of the earth. His is a voice of nature which will never go out in life, and our necessity to echo it does not mean we misunderstand or do not understand him.

Instead, it is possible at the same time to misunderstand and no longer understand the voice of one who, though creating, and in the most accomplished forms, his own organic vision of life, did not endow real and free "movements" of the spirit with his expression, but rather created according to a "pose" or "attitude" of the spirit.

And this "attitude" in itself, usually abstracted from expression, can be overcome, indeed is necessarily overcome, and at a certain point becomes, so to speak, historical, as soon as unexpected agitations of the spirit have displaced the elements of that panorama thus contemplated from a fixed point. Yet, in the movements of the spirit we can never lose interest: the Middle Ages of Dante, not represented according to an attitude of his spirit, as is the eighteenth century of Goldoni, but in the movements of a spirit which need not contemplate its own age because it has all the passions alive in itself, or when it does contemplate, does not stand still a moment because its glance is not attached to time, but from time is attached to eternity and then follows it swiftly and presses it closely, moving it with its doubts and unfolding it with its revelations—this Middle Ages of Dante, just because it is all gathered in the movement of a spirit, can no longer become outmoded; it will always be, in one way or another, echoed in every age. It is possible always, in substance, for every age to receive into itself, one way or another, the spirit of Dante and to feel its perpetual presence; and on the other hand, it is necessary to refer in a certain sense from one's own age to those past times to enjoy the value of the expression of an attitude of the spirit, which can be enjoyed only in its particular flavor and which can not re-echo; it is necessary, in other words, to bring ourselves back to the age of Goldoni.

Goldoni's attitude was good-naturedly satirical: an expression of a wide-awake moral consciousness which remained intact and kept itself whole in reflecting those contingencies it could then satirize, with the satisfaction of feeling them overcome, yet unable to detach them from the spiritual limits of his own time; and hence the good-nature of this satire, which might appear superficial in a period of trial and fundamental upheaval of every established value.

Because of the frankness and transparency of his form, it is and always will be easy to go back to Goldoni, to feel alive, in the life of the representation offered by his spiritual attitude, the rapidity of his wit and the organic wholeness of life so observed and represented. All this is united in a form which, in truth, embalms it forever, together with the freshness and the gaiety of its own expressions, with the happiness of a spirit which created for the joy of creating. The way Goldoni expresses everything will always be a model of correct representation, so fluid and scintillating, so clear and quick, so careful and spontaneous and truly diverting. His propriety of style, not only in dialect, is absolute; nothing is ever said through approximation or in a way that may not be the most frank and savory, just as there is never in conception any emptiness or unbalance in feelings or intellect: conception, elaboration, and expression are exquisitely blended to create a graceful world. Grace, which is one of the most attractive and rarest qualities of human nature, finds in Goldoni its perfect expression, never attained before him; certainly it can not be reached again with such immediacy and in such fullness.

When this fresh expression of life burst on the mummified stage of the Italian theatre and restored to it breath, warmth, and movement, they spoke of a reform. It was the new theatre. Today, can we say that it is old theatre because the spiritual attitude from which it grew is in itself superseded by the change of values with the passing of time?

In art what was created new remains new forever. Goldoni had witty, lively eyes with which he saw anew and created the new.

Any new writer today who copies and does not create, that is, who wears glasses, although in the latest style, and claims that with them he sees the liveliest problems and newest values in his time, if he wears glasses, will copy and will create old theatre.

The new theatre and the old. It is always the same question: of eyes and eyeglasses; of the work of creation and the exercise of copying.

An ape was boasting to a fox, "Can you name an animal so clever and shrewd that I, if I wished, could not imitate?"

And the fox rejoined, "And can you name an animal foolish and stupid enough to want to imitate you?"

ca 1750 This is a little <u>fable of Lessing's</u>, composed at the time of the *c~1630* famous Silesian school led by <u>Martin Opitz</u>, when the German poets endeavored to imitate the graces of the Italian arcadians, bitterly complaining to the good God that they could not become the lap dogs of their ladies.

And as an epilogue to this fable (Lessing's, I repeat, and not mine) in the way of a moral, not for my contemporary playwrights of every land but for the German writers of the eighteenth century, there was the sarcasm of this request, "O authors of my nation, do I have to express myself more clearly?"

A Talk about the Theatre

FEDERICO GARCÍA LORCA

Dear friends, some time ago I made a firm promise to reject any sort of testimonial banquet or celebration that might be made in my modest honor, first of all because I hold that every such affair places a stone on our literary tomb, and secondly, because I have seen that there is nothing more depressing than a formal speech in one's honor nor anything sadder than organized applause, even when in good faith.

Moreover—and this is a secret—I think that banquets and scrolls bring a magical bad luck to the man who receives them, bad luck born from the easy-going attitude of those friends who think, "at last we have done our duty toward him."

A banquet is a meeting of professionals who eat with us, and where we find, in a greater or lesser number, those persons who care for us as little as possible.

For poets and playwrights, instead of testimonials, I would organize attacks and challenges, in which we would be boldly told: "I dare you to do this!" "I bet you aren't capable of expressing a character's fear of the sea!" "I bet you don't dare tell of the desperation of soldiers who are enemies of war!" Necessity and struggle, based on a severe love, temper the artist's soul, which becomes soft and decayed by easy flattery. The theatres are full of fraudulent sirens crowned with hothouse roses, and the public is satisfied and applauds when it beholds hearts of sawdust and mumbled dialogue, but the dramatic poet, if he

"Charla sobre teatro" was presented at a special performance of García Lorca's play *Yerma*, in Madrid in 1935, and is reproduced in his *Obras Completas*, Vol. VIII (Editorial Losada, Buenos Aires, 1949), pp. 153-158. Translated by Haskell M. Block. All rights reserved. Reprinted by permission of New Directions and the Estate of Federico García Lorca.

wishes to escape oblivion, must not forget the fields of roses moistened by the dawn, where peasants labor, and the dove, wounded by a mysterious hunter and dying among the reeds with no one to hear its sighs.

Fleeing from sirens, felicitations, and false greetings, I have accepted no testimonial on the occasion of the première of *Yerma*, but it has been the greatest pleasure of my short life as an author to learn that the theatrical circle of Madrid has demanded a special performance of the play from the great Margarita Xirgu, an actress of pure artistry, luminary of the Spanish theatre and admirable creator of the title role, along with the cast which has so brilliantly accompanied her.

For all of the avid interest in a worthwhile theatrical effort that this event signifies, I express my warmest and most sincere thanks to all of you. I am not speaking tonight as an author or a poet, nor as a simple student of the rich panorama of life, but as a passionate admirer of the theatre of social action. The theatre is one of the most expressive and most useful instruments for the education of a country, and is the barometer that marks its greatness or decline. A theatre that is sensitive and well oriented in all of its branches, from tragedy to vaudeville, can in a few years change the sensibility of a people; and a shattered theatre, in which hoofs substitute for wings, can debase and benumb an entire nation.

The theatre is a school of tears and laughter and a free tribune where men can expose outworn or ambiguous ethics and set forth with living examples eternal patterns of the human heart and human feeling.

A public that does not help and encourage its theatre, if it is not dead, is moribund; just as the theatre which does not embrace the social movement, the historical pulsation, the drama of its peoples and the genuine color of its landscape and its spirit, with laughter and tears, does not have the right to call itself theatre, but a place for games or for that horrible activity called "killing time." I am not referring to any individual nor do I wish to offend anyone; I am not talking about present reality but about a problem without a solution.

Every day, dear friends, I hear discussion of the crisis of the theatre, and I always reflect that the trouble does not lie before our eyes but in the darkest depths of its being. It is not a situation caused by immediate circumstances or works but is deeply rooted; in short, an organizational ill. As long as actors and authors are in the hands of absolutely commercial enterprises which are unrestrained, without literary or state control of any kind, enterprises ignorant of any standards and without security of any sort, actors, authors, and the whole theatre as well will sink lower and lower from one day to the next without any hope of salvation.

The very pleasant light theatre of musical reviews, vaudeville and slapstick comedy, performances of which I am a devoted spectator, can defend itself and even save itself; but the verse theatre, the historical drama and the traditional Spanish musical comedy, will continue to suffer reverses, because these are genres which make great demands, and in which genuine innovations can be made, and there is neither the authority nor the spirit of self-sacrifice to impose them on a public which must be mastered from above and which often has to be contradicted and attacked. The theatre ought to impose itself on the audience and not the other way around. For this, authors and actors must be invested with great authority, even at the price of blood, because the theatre audience is like school children. It reverses the grave and austere teacher who demands and executes justice, and puts cruel needles on the chairs in which timid and obsequious teachers sit, and who neither teach nor let others teach.

It is possible to instruct the audience—note that I say audience, not people—it can be taught, because I have seen people jeer at Debussy and Ravel some years ago, and I have witnessed the clamorous ovations that a popular audience gave to the very works that had been previously rejected. These composers were imposed on the audience by a standard of authority superior to that of the ordinary public, as was also the case with Wedekind in Germany, Pirandello in Italy, and many others.

This has to be done for the good of the theatre and for the glory and rank of the actors. They must maintain a dignified attitude, certain that such an attitude will be more than adequately recompensed. To do otherwise is to tremble with fear behind the wings and to kill the fantasy, imagination and grace of the theatre, which is always, always an art and always will be a sublime art, despite an epoch which called art everything it disliked, in order to corrupt the atmosphere, to destroy poetry and make of the stage a haven of ruthless violence.

Art above all. The noblest of arts, and you, dear members of the cast, artists above all. Artists from head to foot, since through love and your vocation you have mounted the simulated and painful world of the stage. Artists by occupation and preoccupation. From the simplest to the most elaborate theatre the word "Art" must be written, in large halls and in dressing rooms; otherwise we will have to write the word "Commerce" or some other that I dare not say. And also let us have orderliness, discipline, sacrifice and love.

I do not want to give you a lecture, because I am the one who needs a lecture. My words are dictated by enthusiasm and assurance. I am under no delusion. I have meditated long and dispassionately on these thoughts, and like a good Andalusian, I have the secret of cool control because I am of ancient blood. I know that he is not in possession of truth who exclaims "Today! Today!", eating his bread close to the fire, but rather he who serenely gazes in the distance at the first gleam of the country dawn.

I know that he is wrong who shouts "Now! Now! Right now!" with his eyes fixed on the little windows in the box offices, but not he who says, "Tomorrow! Tomorrow!" and feels the coming of the new life which hovers over the world.

Discourse on the Theatre

JEAN GIRAUDOUX

Dear comrades, only orators are interrupted by emotion. The pharynx of the writer, as it is a tool of secondary value, remains open in moments when that of lawyers or politicians would close. If, therefore, I respond to our president in my clearest voice, do not believe that I am any the less aware of his kind words and your reception. Through his friendly intervention, you have granted me the role of presiding over the annual meeting which places on the faces of several generations the same mask, not of youth, alas, but of childhood; to preside over friends who meet again after thirty years of separation, and over colleagues who knew each other only by name and who are suddenly found seated together, a symphony of shouts and laughter which we have not heard since the days of the school dining hall, and which gave rise to the same echoes on the rue de Poitiers as on the Avenue de Déols: Duchâteau, Malinet, Bailly, Delacou, Naudin, Berthon. . . . Believe me, I am profoundly grateful to you for this event.

I would have limited myself to an expression of this satisfaction and gratitude if during this past week some of my friends had not asked me, in letters and personally, to make my response less brief. As fellow classmates, they have followed the effort which I have been making in the theatre during the past three years. They have been surprised to find that this effort has recently provoked the most opposite reactions among critics who

The "Discours sur le Théâtre" was delivered by Giraudoux at the banquet of the Paris Association of Former Students of the Lycée of Châteauroux on November 19, 1931. Printed in Jean Giraudoux, *Littérature*, Editions Bernard Grasset, Paris, 1941, pp. 231-241. Translated by Haskell M. Block.

generally agree. They would like me to present here an explanation of such divergence of opinion, and I will do so gladly. Do not politicians select precisely such friendly gatherings as this to expound their aims or to justify their actions? It seems to restore to their ambitions a color and a freshness which they quite conceivably may have lost, by plunging them once again into this bath of youthfulness. Why shouldn't writers imitate them? Who could possibly better understand and lend strength to a man of letters than those who opened the classics for the first time in the same editions, recited in the same classrooms, and committed their first barbarisms and grammatical errors with the same French or Latin words?

Besides, I am not completely sure that I shall not be presenting a political, or at least a social, discourse. The subject of the theatre and its plays, which has been of major and at times decisive importance in human history, has lost none of its significance at a time when the average person sees his spare time for leisure and amusement increased enormously as his working day is reduced to seven or eight hours. The stage is the only form of a nation's spiritual and artistic education. It is the only evening activity that is good for old men as well as for young adults, the only way by which the most humble and unlettered public can enter into direct contact with the greatest of conflicts and create for itself a lay religion, a liturgy and saints, feelings and passions. There are some persons who have dreams, but for those who do not dream there is the theatre. The lucidity of the French people in no way implies its rejection of great spiritual forces. The cult of the dead, this cult of heroes which dominates the French people proves conclusively that it loves to see great persons, persons who are at once near and unapproachable, living its humble and definite life amid nobility and the indefinite. Its cult of equality also is flattered by this model of equality before the emotion which constitutes the theatre when the curtain rises, an equality surpassed only by that of the corn field at harvest time. If it is admitted but once a year, in the midst of our national holiday, to the free matinée of the 14th of July, as befits our democracy, to live for a few hours at the

Odéon and at the Comédie-Française with kings and queens, with movements as kings and passions queens, believe me when I tell you that the public is not to be blamed for it. Wherever it may find an alternative to the mediocrity of the stage, it hurries. In the few hallowed places as yet unpolluted by the disease of the scurrilous and the easy, masses of spectators from all classes of the population are crowded together, listening respectfully to the most obscure of the works of Aeschylus or Sophocles, it mattering very little that they grasp its details, for the tragic works on them as a curative of gold and the sun. In the mask of costume, the tapestry of the set, the undergrowth of words, this assembly of charming Epicureans and of happy owners of hunting licenses—which generally constitutes an audience in southern France—follows with anguish and passion the serpentine meandering of the invisible hydra which has arisen from the most magnificent antiquity; for it is in the brightest and purest of epochs that the monsters of the soul have their lair. Saints at Orange! Do southern cities alone suddenly give emotion and intelligence to spectators who just as suddenly in other places become devotees of the café concert and the talking film? Is it that the open sky restores the primitive nobility of an audience, and that under a roof the Frenchman sinks again into vulgarity? No, it is that around these privileged enclosures the public is imbued with respect for the theatre, that it is urged by its leaders and even by municipalities to cultivate an instinctive and exact conception of the theatre. . . . In Paris it loses it; it has lost it.

It has lost it because instead of respecting the theatre and raising oneself to its level, a few men of the theatre have claimed to appeal only to its pliability and its meanness. Incomprehension if not outright scorn of the public has been the axiom of a definite part of the Paris stage. All that counts is to please by the most common and basest of means. As the French language, when spoken and written correctly, itself resists this blackmail and obeys only those whom it respects, it is against the language that this offensive has been led, and for plays in which it is not insulted and deformed, some have found an epithet tantamount, it would seem, to the worst of insults: that of literary plays. If, in your work, your characters avoid this enfeeblement of expression with which some writers have come to mark even their play on sounds or their monosyllables; if, through the study of character, the detail of explanation, you depart no matter how little from this platform improvisation which represents the ideal play for more than one director, you hear it said at once, more or perhaps less crudely—for such insults are always expressed with caution—that you are not a man of the theatre but a writer of literature. You learn, then, for your guidance, that while every domain of activity in France is open to literature, there are exactly two areas formally barred to it: the theatre and the cinema. It is clear why directors should have this conviction. They are in charge of an enterprise; they have to lead it to success and not to a deficit; the stinginess of the government prevents them from being educators or philanthropists. Their art of poetry stops at their balance sheet. It is also true that the platform theatre which has become our theatre of the boulevards can produce models, perishable, like all that is gesture and not language, but models all the same. Certain critics, however, themselves men of letters, undergo a fit of impatience before a play that is written and not spoken, and before launching against it an attack which might on other grounds be justified, take not the slightest trouble to inform their reader in what noble enclosure this tourney is held; and this is less allowable. And when some of them, vaguely aware of their wrongdoing, tell you, to excuse themselves: "What a dull play, but how we will enjoy reading it!" they are judging themselves, for this statement gives its true meaning to the applause they lavished the night before on another play: "What a successful play! How we will enjoy not reading it!"

You understand, of course, that I have no intention of undertaking here an appraisal of these drama critics. Their probity is absolute; their sincerity is unfortunately without question. And insofar as their love of the theatre is concerned, there is once again no basis for distinguishing them from those famous predecessors of whom Antoine was the most illustrious, and from the numerous youths who work as hard as they can to bring about a literary theatre. Nor is the bad faith and the inconsequence of their remarks of any importance, nor the uncertain taste revealed in their articles which ought, none the less, to connect them to literature. It makes little difference that the drama critic of one of our most important morning papers, reviewing a play wherein he condemns its questionable style, calls one Jewess devoted to another an "Estheromane" and an effeminate military aide "the tent-keeper" of Holophernes. It makes little difference that the poetess who personifies for us delicacy and modesty states, in her review of a play in which the action takes place at Bethulia and in which the language does not seem quite pure, that she was "Borethuled" by it, and calls pure virgins "girls who want to break their jugs." The pun is perhaps the ideal form of expression for the excitable purist shocked by Gongorisms. But the harm is not there. The harm comes from the fact that this variety of critics represents an outmoded variety, the fashionable sort, and we no longer have a literature catering to fashion any more than a fashionable society. The harm—I mean, of course, the good thing about it all—is that the theatre, the novel, even criticism, instead of serving as mere accessories of a peaceful and superficial middle-class life, have become once more, in our age as in every age of fullness and anxiety, tools of primary necessity. This dismemberment of the body of literature into several fragments, performed in a happy century for the benefit of salons and parties, and which had brought novelists, journalists, playwrights, and philosophers to form so many hostile and independent cliques, no longer has any justification. The man of letters feels perfectly at home in the theatre, in the newspaper, in the advertising office: he has invaded all of these realms. The heart of literature has been rediscovered, this magnet which will bring once more into a single unit so many scattered limbs, and this heart is the writer, it is writing. Every great upheaval of minds and manners diminishes the importance of literary *genres* in themselves but increases a hundred fold the role of the writer and gives him back his universality. Our epoch no longer demands works from the man of letters—the streets and courtyards are filled with such useless furniture—it demands from him above all else a language. It no longer expects the writer to play the fool to the happy king, relating his truths in soothing and successful novels or plays, critiques which are as contemptible as they are flattering; the age expects him to reveal his truth to it and, so that it may organize his thought and his sensibility, to entrust it with the secret which the writer alone possesses: that of style. That is what it also demands from the theatre. The protests of those who do not care to distinguish between theatrical works aiming at the formation of the public and those which seek only to flatter or to please it no longer count for anything, for the public is against them and with us. The public at the theatre, listening to a text, has absolutely no experience of what the half-learned call boredom. Its seat at the theatre has the extra-territoriality of an embassy in an ancient or heroic kingdom, in the domain of illogic and fantasy, and it intends to preserve its solemn character. The affection which the public holds for the theatre in verse is the expression of this veneration for vocabulary and style. It admires in verse the work well done, the consciousness and care which it ascribes to the poet. But when a writer reveals that his prose is not flabby, not low, not obscene, not easy, it asks only to believe him, and is carried away when it suddenly sees, in place of the substitute coin which marks the theatrical style, the actor and the actress exchanging words which disclose that a people's most precious possession, its language, is laden with gold.

These, dear friends, are the reflections which the theatre of today can inspire in a writer. If they have been expressed somewhat briefly, I ask you above all not to blame those among you who are responsible for them. I would have given them to you sooner or later of my own accord, for despite the advances which Delphi, Orange, and Munich have made to me, Châteauroux remains my favorite theatre town, ever since that evening when I was in the sixth grade, when we were lined up in the way we used to be to go to the chapel or the bath, and were led for the first time to the theatre. Silvain was playing the role of aged

Horace, and every adolescent in the province of Berry waited passionately for the words, "Let him die," and the stage took on an unexpected grandeur for the curtain did not work and was held up with pikes, by two firemen of Châteauroux in uniform.

The Eternal Law of the Dramatist

JEAN GIRAUDOUX

Two rules govern, if I may speak in this way, the eternal law of
the dramatist.

The first consecrates the sorry and somewhat ridiculous position of the author in relation to those of his characters that he
has created and given to the theatre. To the extent that he finds
a character to be docile, familiar, belonging to him, to that extent the character becomes foreign and indifferent to the author
once it is given to the public. The first actor to play the part
constitutes the first in a series of reincarnations in which the
character becomes more and more distant from its author and
steals away from him forever. This is also true of the play as
a whole. After the first performance it belongs to the actors, and
the author who haunts the wings becomes a sort of ghost, detested by the stagehands if he listens or is indiscreet; after the
hundredth performance, especially if the play is a good one, it
belongs to the public. The truth is that the playwright really
owns only his bad plays. The independence of those of his characters who have succeeded is complete; the life they lead on tour
or in America is a constant denial of their filial obligations, and,
while the heroes of your novels follow you everywhere calling
you Father or Daddy, dramatic characters among those whom
you meet by chance, as has happened to me in Carcassonne or in
Los Angeles, have become total strangers. To a large extent it
is to punish them for this independence that Goethe, Claudel,
and many others have made new versions of plays with their
favorite heroines. In vain. The new Margaret, the new Helen,

From Jean Giraudoux, *Visitations*, Bernard Grasset, Paris, 1952, pp. 115-
122. Translated by Haskell M. Block.

the new Violaine were no less prompt to abandon them. I once went to a performance of *The Tidings Brought to Mary* with Claudel and, on that occasion at least, this situation worked in my favor: the play, I observed, was infinitely more mine than it was his.

How many authors are obliged to search in an actress or actor for the memory of the reflection of a daughter or son who has gone off—much as parents, in a more everyday setting, must do in a son-in-law or daughter-in-law. . . . On the terrace of the Weber, in the generals' vestibule, on the lawn of the country house of a famous actress, how many of these couples have we met: Feydeau and Cassive, Jules Renard and Suzanne Deprès, Réjane and Maurice Donnay, the woman just a little absent-minded, the man attentive and absorbed in memories, loquacious and questioning, talking about the woman who was not there.

The second law, a corollary and the reverse of the first, consecrates the wonderful position of the dramatic author in relation to his epoch and its events, and indicates his role. And here, if I wish to be truthful, I surely must relieve my colleagues and myself of any false modesty. This narrator, who in the play is but a voice, without personality, without responsibility, but who is also an historian and an avenger, exists in the age as flesh and bone; he is the dramatic author himself. For every playwright worthy of the name, one should be able to say, when his work is performed: "Add the archangel to your play!" It is vain to believe that a year or a century can find the resonance and the elevation which are necessary, in the long run, to this pathetic debate and this sorry effort which is each moment of our passage on earth, if there were not a spokesman for the tragedy or the drama to fix its height and to plumb its foundation and vault. Tragedy and drama are the confession this army of salvation and damnation which is humanity must also make in public, without reticence and in its highest pitch, for the echo of its voice is more distinct and more real than the voice itself. We should not delude ourselves on this point. The relationship between the theatre and religious solemnity is evident, and it is not by chance that in front of our cathedrals there used to be dramatic performances at every occasion. The theatre is at its best in the church courtyard. It is there that the public goes to the theater on holiday nights, to the illuminated confession of its dwarfed and gigantic destinies. Calderón is humanity confessing its desire for eternity, Corneille its dignity, Racine its weakness, Shakespeare its passion for life, Claudel its condition of sin and salvation, Goethe its humanity, Kleist its lightning. Epochs are in accord with themselves only if the crowd comes into these radiant confessionals which are the theatres or the arenas, and as much as possible, in its most brilliant confessional dress, in order to increase the solemnity of the event, to listen to its own confessions of cowardice and sacrifice, of hate and passion. And what if the crowd too should exclaim: "Add the prophet to the play!" For there is no theatre which is not prophecy. Not this false divination which gives names and dates, but true prophecy, that which reveals to men these surprising truths: that the living must live, that the living must die, that autumn must follow summer, spring follow winter, that there are four elements, that there is happiness, that there are innumerable miseries, that life is a reality, that it is a dream, that man lives in peace, that man lives on blood; in short, those things they will never know. Such is the theatre, the public restoration of these incredible prodigies whose visions will disturb and overwhelm the night of the onlookers, but whose dawn, no doubt—my faith rejoices in it— to make the author's mission an everyday reality, will have already diluted in them the lesson and the memory. This is dramatic representation, the spectator's sudden consciousness of the permanent condition of this living and indifferent humanity: passion and death.

To Jean Giraudoux

JEAN ANOUILH

Fortunate are those young men who have had masters!

Fortunate are the nervous youngsters who went and rang doorbells and received with flushed faces the encouraging word from the man whom they admired!

I grew up without any masters; in the years around 1928, I had a warm place in my heart for Claudel and I carried dog-eared copies of Shaw and Pirandello in my pockets; and yet, I was all alone. Alone with the anguish of one soon to be twenty years old, with a love for the theatre, and all the awkwardness of youth. Who would divulge to me the secret in those days in which only well-made plays were performed? Musset, Marivaux reread a thousand times? They were too far off. They were from an era already fabulous in which spoken French still had periods and commas, from an era in which the very sentences danced. And yet, there was a secret, a secret doubtless lost for a long time and which I was much too small ever to find again by myself. Eighteen years old! and my studies which were already becoming hazy, and a livelihood to earn somehow, and this anguish, these stiff fingers. Of course, Claudel before me was to have found the secret again or rather he had found another one, one suited only to him; but he was like a great inaccessible statue, a saint of wood upon a mountain whom one could ask for nothing.

It was then that an incomparable springtime came, warming and bringing into flower the Avenue Montaigne.

In all of my life, I believe that I shall never again see such

Jean Anouilh's essay, "A Jean Giraudoux," first appeared in *La Chronique de Paris*, I (February, 1944), 1-3. It is reprinted in English in *The Tulane Drama Review*, III (May, 1959), 3-5. Translated by Arthur Evans.

chestnut trees, such balminess in the air. There were evenings when, in those lights which tinted the leaves above with blue, I pressed close to the gods, when I joined in the bustling throng of long automobiles, of women in evening clothes, in that sudden perfection which everything took on for me in that corner of Paris.

Oh, the exits of the audience from *Siegfried* . . . Dear Giraudoux, who will tell you now, since I never dared or wished to tell you, what strange encounters of despair and the harshest joy, of pride and the tenderest humility, took place in this young man who stumbled down from the upper gallery of the *Comédie des Champs-Elysées?*

Because of you that avenue and that thoroughfare, isolated by invisible signs in the midst of a detestable quarter, will always remain for me the streets of my village. Nowadays, I never pass through this landscape, zigzagging between the white barriers of the war and my memories, without being inundated with happiness.

The theatre, my life of beauty (oh the terrace of the "Francis" where Jouvet and Renoir would sit and drink and behind which I imagined God knows what sort of lavish display!), poetry, indeed, the inaccessible, caused me to choose my domicile between the Métro Alma and the Plaza Hotel, in that almost spa-like elegance, with its women in diamonds in the warm shadows, its men in white dress shirts. In the heat of a precocious summer, what château suddenly loomed forth from amid the middle-class barracks, and what entertainment was presented there which compelled this young fellow to remain there, without the strength to leave, after everyone else had left?

Even though others have found their poetry in the quiet streets of a sleepy town, along the banks of a still lake, under the vaults of a church or forest, in a poetic setting, my poetry was to have its *rendez-vous* with me, because of you, in that Parisian landscape for rich foreigners with its accessory figures scarcely suited to please me.

I still know *Siegfried* by heart, dear Giraudoux. Did I tell you that at the only dinner which I had with you, the only time when

I was with you for more than five minutes? Did I tell you that I can still imitate all the voices? Boverio as Zelten, "It is you, dark-skinned brachycephalic one, with too many spectacles and too many woolen waistcoats?" and Bouquet, the poor Bouquet, "Son of Arminius, Glutton of carnage, it is I . . ." and Jouvet-Fontgeloy, whose accent of a "Hussard general of death" you'd swear was authentic, and their patron—just a minute now—"is never far away." And Renoir and Bogaert and Valentine and the inimitable Simon himself as the customs inspector.

Dear Giraudoux, I didn't tell you something else, it was the evening of *Siegfried* that I understood. As a consequence, I was to enter into a long night from which I have not yet completely emerged, from which, perhaps, I shall never emerge, but it is because of those spring evenings in 1928 when I, the only spectator, wept, even at the amusing dialogue, that I have been able to move somewhat out of myself.

Then came *Amphitryon, Intermezzo*, both farther from me; then, irritated with the man who produced them and intransigent as innocence is wont to be, I no longer saw your plays performed. I would read them, overwhelmed, without opera *décor*, without glitter, without excess of magic tricks, without that imposing air of gala which your *premières* always managed to take on somewhat too lavishly. I would talk about them with Pitoëff— my other master, but with whom I was on familiar terms—who regretted so much your admirable *Electre* and then, finally, I experienced that tender despair a last time with *Ondine*.

When Jouvet—detested (I was his secretary) and then suddenly pardoned for so much just nobleness of spirit—lay down in his black armor upon that long gray stone, a despair rent me which I shall never forget.

It was not only too beautiful, it not only made ridiculous everything I had wanted to do, it was tender, solemn, and definitive like a farewell. I had a very certain feeling about it: the farewell of Hans to Ondine took on the meaning of another farewell which wrenched my heart. It was the time of the phony war and we dreamed about lives in danger. I believed, naively, that this mysterious farewell concerned me.

Dear Giraudoux, it was you whom I was leaving, owing you so much without ever having told you, having known you so little and so well.

I am happy, at least, that at the end of that dinner, last winter, where for the first time I was with you for more than five minutes, and where I still said nothing to you, I took hold of your overcoat and I helped you put it on. This is something I never do, and I surprised myself in doing it and in fixing your coat collar so that you would be warmer. Then, this familiarity coming from I know not where suddenly bothered me and I left you. . . .

But now I am happy that I served you, at least once, as schoolboys used to serve their masters, in exchange for that evening of *Siegfried*.

Theatre for Pleasure or Theatre for Learning?

BERTOLT BRECHT

When anyone spoke of modern theatre a few years ago, he mentioned the Moscow, the New York, or the Berlin theatre. He may also have spoken of a particular production of Jouvet's in Paris, of Cochran's in London, or the Habima performance of *The Dybbuk*, which, in fact, belonged to Russian theatre, since it was directed by Vakhtangov; but, by and large, there were only three capitals as far as modern theatre was concerned.

The Russian, the American, and the German theatres were very different from one another, but they were alike in being modern, i.e., in introducing technical and artistic innovations. In a certain sense they even developed stylistic similarities, probably because technique is international (not only the technique directly required for the stage, but also that which exerts an influence on it, the film, for example) and because the cities in question were great progressive cities in great industrial countries. Most recently, the Berlin theatre seemed to have taken the lead among the most advanced capitalist countries. For a time, what was common to modern theatre found there its strongest and, for the moment, its most mature expression.

The last phase of the Berlin theatre, which as I said only revealed in its purest form the direction in which modern theatre was developing, was the so-called epic theatre. What was known as the "*Zeitstück*"—the play dealing with current problems— or the Piscator theatre, or the didactic play, all belong to epic theatre.

"Vergnügungstheater oder Lehrtheater?" was written around 1936. It is reprinted in Bertolt Brecht, *Schriften zum Theater*, Suhrkamp Verlag, Frankfurt am Main, 1957, pp. 60-73. Translated by Edith Anderson in *Mainstream*, Vol. XI (June, 1958), pp. 1-9. Slight revisions have been made by the editors.

The expression "epic theatre" seemed self-contradictory to many people, since according to the teachings of Aristotle the epic and the dramatic forms of presenting a story were considered basically different from one another. The difference between the two forms was by no means merely seen in the fact that one was performed by living people while the other made use of a book—epic works like those of Homer and the Minnesingers of the Middle Ages were likewise theatrical performances, and dramas like Goethe's *Faust* or Byron's *Manfred* admittedly achieved their greatest effect as books. Aristotle's teachings themselves distinguished the dramatic from the epic form as a difference in construction, whose laws were dealt with under two different branches of aesthetics. This construction depended on the different way in which the works were presented to the public, either on the stage or through a book, but nevertheless, apart from that, "the dramatic" could also be found in the epic works and "the epic" in dramatic works. The bourgeois novel in the last century considerably developed "the dramatic," which meant the strong centralization of plot and an organic interdependence of the separate parts. "The dramatic" is characterized by a certain passion in the tone of the exposition and a working out of the collision of forces. The epic writer, Döblin, gave an excellent characterization when he said that the epic, in contrast to the dramatic, could practically be cut up with a scissors into single pieces, each of which could stand alone.

I do not intend to discuss here in what way the contrasts between the epic and the dramatic, long regarded as irreconcilable, lost their rigidity; let it suffice to point out that technical achievements alone enabled the stage to incorporate narrative elements into dramatic presentations. The potentialities of projection, the film, the greater facility in changing sets through machinery, completed the equipment of the stage and did so at a moment when the most important human events could no longer be so simply portrayed as through personification of the moving forces or through subordinating the characters to invisible, metaphysical powers.

To make the events understandable, the environment of human activity had to be given great and "significant" value.

Of course this environment had been shown in plays before, not, however, as an independent element but only from the viewpoint of the main figure of the drama. It rose out of the hero's reaction to it. It was seen as a storm may be "seen" if you observe on the sea a ship spreading its sails and the sails bellying. But in the epic theatre it was now to appear as an independent element.

The stage began to narrate. The narrator no longer vanished with the fourth wall. Not only did the background make its own comment on stage happenings through large screens which evoked other events occurring at the same time in other places, documenting or contradicting statements by characters through phrases projected onto a screen, lending tangible, concrete statistics to abstract discussions, providing facts and figures for happenings which were plastic but unclear in their meaning; the actors no longer threw themselves completely into their roles but maintained a certain distance from the character performed by them, even distinctly inviting criticism.

Nothing permitted the audience any more to lose itself through simple identification, uncritically (and without any practical consequences), in the experiences of the characters on the stage. The presentation exposed the subject matter and the happenings to a process of alienation. Alienation was required to make things understood. When things are "self-evident," understanding is simply dispensed with.

The "natural" had to be given an element of the conspicuous. Only in this way could the laws of cause and effect become plain. Characters had to behave as they did behave, and, at the same time, they had to be capable of behaving otherwise.

These were great changes.

The spectator in the dramatic theatre says: Yes, I have felt that too.—That's how I am.—That is only natural.—That will always be so.—This person's suffering shocks me because he has no way out.—This is great art: everything in it is self-evident.—I weep with the weeping, I laugh with the laughing.

The spectator in the epic theatre says: I wouldn't have thought that.—People shouldn't do things like that.—That's extremely odd, almost unbelievable.—This has to stop.—This person's suffering shocks me, because there might be a way out for him.—This is great art: nothing in it is self-evident.—I laugh over the weeping, I weep over the laughing.

DIDACTIC THEATRE

The stage began to instruct.

Oil, inflation, war, social struggles, the family, religion, wheat, the meat-packing industry became subjects for theatrical portrayal. Choruses informed the audience about facts it did not know. Films displayed events from all over the world. Projections provided statistical data. As the "background" came to the fore, the actions of the characters became exposed to criticism. Wrong and right actions were exhibited. People were shown who knew what they were doing, and other people were shown who did not know. The theatre became a matter for philosophers —for that sort of philosopher, to be sure, who wanted not only to explain the world but also to change it. For this reason, the theatre philosophized; for this reason, it instructed. And what became of entertainment? Were the audiences put back in school, treated as illiterates? Were they to pass examinations? Be given marks?

It is the general opinion that a very decided difference exists between learning and being entertained. The former may be useful, but only the latter is pleasant. Thus we have to defend the epic theatre against a suspicion that it must be an extremely unpleasant, a joyless, indeed a wearing business.

Well, we can actually only say that the contrast between learning and being entertained does not necessarily exist by nature, it has not always existed, and it need not always exist.

Undoubtedly, the kind of learning we did in school, in training for a profession or the like, is a laborious business. But consider under what circumstances and for what purpose it is done.

It is, in fact, a purchase. Knowledge is simply a commodity. It is acquired for the purpose of being resold. All those who have grown too old for school have to pursue knowledge secretly, so to speak, because anybody who admits he still has to study depreciates himself as one who knows too little. Apart from that, the utility of learning is very much limited by factors over which the student has no control. There is unemployment, against which no knowledge protects. There is the division of labor, which makes comprehensive knowledge unnecessary and impossible. Often, those who study make the effort only when they see that no other effort offers a possibility of getting ahead. There is not much knowledge that procures power, but there is much knowledge which is only procured through power.

Learning means something very different to different strata of society. There are strata of people who cannot conceive of any improvement in conditions; conditions seem good enough to them. Whatever may happen to petroleum, they make a profit out of it. And they feel, after all, that they are getting rather old. They can scarcely expect many more years of life. So why continue to learn? They have already spoken their last word! But there are also strata of people who have not yet "had their turn," who are discontented with the way things are, who have an immense practical interest in learning, who want orientation badly, who know they are lost without learning—these are the best and most ambitious learners. Such differences also exist among nations and peoples. Thus the lust for learning is dependent on various things; in short, there is such a thing as thrilling learning, joyous and militant learning.

If learning could not be delightful, then the theatre, by its very structure, would not be in a position to instruct.

Theatre remains theatre, even when it is didactic theatre, and insofar as it is good theatre, it will entertain.

THEATRE AND SCIENCE

But what has science to do with art? We know very well that science can be diverting, but not everything that diverts belongs to the theatre.

153

I have often been told when I pointed out the inestimable services that modern science, properly utilized, can render to art, especially to the theatre, that art and science were two valuable but completely different fields of human activity. This is a dreadful platitude, of course, and the best thing to do is admit at once that it is quite right, like most platitudes. Art and science operate in very different ways—agreed. Still, I must admit—bad as this may sound—that I cannot manage as an artist without making use of certain sciences. This may make many people seriously doubt my artistic ability. They are accustomed to regarding poets as unique, almost unnatural beings who, with truly godlike infallibility, perceive things that others can only perceive through the greatest efforts and hard work. Naturally, it is unpleasant to have to admit not being one of those so endowed. But it must be admitted. It must also be denied that these admitted scientific efforts have anything to do with some pardonable avocation indulged in the evening after work is done. Everyone knows that Goethe also went in for natural science, Schiller for history, presumably—this is the charitable assumption—as a sort of hobby. I would not simply accuse these two of having needed the science for their poetic labors, nor would I use them to excuse myself, but I must say I need the sciences. And I must even admit that I regard suspiciously all sorts of people who I know do not keep abreast of science, who, in other words, sing as the birds sing, or as they imagine the birds sing. This does not mean that I would reject a nice poem about the taste of a flounder or the pleasure of a boating party just because the author had not studied gastronomy or navigation. But I think that unless every resource is employed toward understanding the great, complicated events in the world of man, they cannot be seen adequately for what they are.

Let us assume that we want to portray great passions or events which influence the fates of peoples. Such a passion today might be the drive for power. Supposing that a poet "felt" this drive and wanted to show someone striving for power—how could he absorb into his own experience the extremely complicated mechanism within which the struggle for power today takes place? If his hero is a political man, what are the workings of politics; if he is a business man, what are the workings of business? And then there are poets who are much less passionately interested in any individual's drive for power than in business affairs and politics as such! How are they to acquire the necessary knowledge? They will scarcely find out enough by going around and keeping their eyes open, although that is at least better than rolling their eyes in a fine frenzy! The establishment of a newspaper like *Der Völkische Beobachter* or a business like Standard Oil is a rather complicated matter, and these things are not simply absorbed through the pores. Psychology is an important field for the dramatist. It is supposed that while an ordinary person may not be in a position to discover, without special instruction, what makes a man commit murder, certainly a writer ought to have the "inner resources" to be able to give a picture of a murderer's mental state. The assumption is that you only need look into yourself in such a case; after all, there is such a thing as imagination. . . . For a number of reasons I can no longer abandon myself in this amiable hope of managing so comfortably. I cannot find in myself alone all the motives which, as we learn from newspapers and scientific reports, are discovered in human beings. No more than any judge passing sentence am I able to imagine adequately, unaided, the mental state of a murderer. Modern psychology, from psychoanalysis to behaviorism, provides me with insights which help me to form a quite different judgment of the case, especially when I take into consideration the findings of sociology, and do not ignore economics or history. You may say: this is getting complicated. I must answer, it *is* complicated. Perhaps I can talk you into agreeing with me that a lot of literature is extremely primitive; yet you will ask in grave concern: Wouldn't such an evening in the theatre be a pretty alarming business? The answer to that is: No.

Whatever knowledge may be contained in a literary work, it must be completely converted into literature. In its transmuted form, it gives the same type of satisfaction as any literary work. And although it does not provide that satisfaction found in science as such, a certain inclination to penetrate more deeply into the nature of things, a desire to make the world controllable, are necessary to ensure enjoyment of literary works generated by this era of great discoveries and inventions.

IS THE EPIC THEATRE PERHAPS A "MORAL INSTITUTION"?

According to Friedrich Schiller, the theatre should be a moral institution. When Schiller posed this demand, it scarcely occurred to him that by moralizing from the stage he might drive the audience out of the theatre. In his day the audience had no objection to moralizing. Only later on did Friedrich Nietzsche abuse him as the moral trumpeter of Säckingen. To Nietzsche a concern with morality seemed a dismal affair; to Schiller it seemed completely gratifying. He knew of nothing more entertaining and satisfying than to propagate ideals. The bourgeoisie was just establishing the concept of the nation. To furnish your house, show off your new hat, present your bills for payment is highly gratifying. But to speak of the decay of your house, to have to sell your old hat, and pay the bills yourself is a truly dismal affair, and that was how Friedrich Nietzsche saw it a century later. He had nothing good to say of morality nor, consequently, of the other Friedrich.

Many people also attacked the epic theatre, claiming it was too moralistic. Yet moral utterances were secondary in the epic theatre. Its intention was less to moralize than to study. And it did study, but then came the rub: the moral of the story. Naturally, we cannot claim that we began making studies just because studying was so much fun and not for any concrete reason, or that the results of our studies then took us completely by surprise. Undoubtedly there were painful discrepancies in the world around us, conditions that were hard to bear, conditions of a kind hard to bear not only for moral reasons. Hunger, cold, and hardship are not only burdensome for moral reasons. And the purpose of our investigation was not merely to arouse moral misgivings about certain conditions (although such misgivings might easily be felt, if not by every member of the audience; such misgivings, for example, were seldom felt by those who profited by the conditions in question). The purpose of our investigation was to reveal the means by which those onerous conditions could be done away with. We were not speaking on behalf of morality but on behalf of the wronged. These are really two different things, for moral allusions are often used in telling the wronged that they must put up with their situation. For such moralists, people exist for morality, not morality for people.

Nevertheless it can be deduced from these remarks to what extent and in what sense the epic theater is a moral institution.

CAN EPIC THEATRE BE PERFORMED ANYWHERE?

From the standpoint of style, the epic theatre is nothing especially new. In its character of show, of demonstration, and its emphasis on the artistic, it is related to the ancient Asian theatre. The medieval mystery play, and also the classical Spanish and Jesuit theatres, showed an instructive tendency.

Those theatre forms corresponded to certain tendencies of their time and disappeared with them. The modern epic theatre is also linked to definite tendencies. It can by no means be performed anywhere. Few of the great nations today are inclined to discuss their problems in the theatre. London, Paris, Tokyo, and Rome maintain their theatres for quite different purposes. Only in a few places, and not for long, have circumstances been favorable to an epic, instructive theatre. In Berlin, fascism put a violent stop to the development of such a theatre.

Besides a certain technical standard, it presupposes a powerful social movement which has an interest in the free discussion of vital problems, the better to solve them, and which can defend this interest against all opposing tendencies.

The epic theatre is the broadest and most far-reaching experiment in great modern theatre, and it has to overcome all the enormous difficulties that all vital forces in the area of politics, philosophy, science, and art have to overcome.

Observations on Mother Courage

BERTOLT BRECHT

I

Mother Courage Presented in Two Ways

In the usual manner of stage presentation, which produces a feeling of identification with the principal character, the spectator of *Mother Courage* (according to the testimony of many) comes to enjoy a peculiar pleasure: a triumph over the indestructibility of a vital person who has been visited by the tribulations and injuries of war. The active participation of Mother Courage in the war is not taken seriously; it is a means of support, possibly the only one. Apart from this motive of participation—indeed, in spite of it—the effect is similar to that in the case of *The Good Soldier Schweik*, where—of course, in a comic sphere—the spectator triumphs with Schweik over the plans for his sacrifice by the major belligerent Powers. The similar effect in the case of Mother Courage is, however, of far less social value, because her very participation, as indirectly as it may be presented, is not deliberated. In actuality, this effect is even quite negative. Mother Courage appears principally as a mother and, like Niobe, she is unable to protect her children from the doom

"Observations on *Mother Courage*" consists of three selections. The first, "*Mutter Courage* in zweifacher Art dargestellt," was first published in *Aufbau*, Vol. XI (1955), pp. 1021-22, and is reprinted in Bertolt Brecht, *Schriften zum Theater*, Suhrkamp Verlag, Frankfurt, 1957, pp. 205-207. It was written in 1951. The second selection, "Notes to *Mother Courage*," is from Brecht's "Anmerkungen," *Versuche* 9, Suhrkamp Verlag, Berlin, 1950, pp. 81 and 83. The third selection is from *Theaterarbeit*, VVV Dresdner Verlag, Dresden, 1952, pp. 253-254, and is part of remarks on the play made by Brecht during an interview. All translations are by Herman Salinger.

of war. Her trade as a dealer and the manner in which she practices it, give her at most something "realistically not ideal," without, however, taking from the war anything of its character of doom. It is, of course, here too, purely negative, but in the end she survives it, even though marred. In the face of this, Helene Weigel, employing a technique which prevented complete empathy, treated the dealer's occupation not as a merely natural, but as an historical one, that is to say, as belonging to an historical and *past* epoch, and the war as the best time for business. Here, too, trade was to be taken for granted as a means of support, but a dirty one after all, from which Mother Courage drank death. The trader-mother became a great living contradiction and it was this that defaced and deformed her, to the point of making her unrecognizable. In the scene on the battlefield, which is generally omitted in the usual manner of presentation, she was really a hyena; she brought out the shirts only because she saw the hate of her daughter and feared the use of force, and, cursing, she flung herself like a tiger upon the soldier with the cloak. After the maiming of her daughter, she damned the war with a sincerity just as deep as that with which she praised it in the scene immediately following. Thus, she gave expression to opposites in all their abruptness and irreconcilability. The rebellion of her daughter against her (at the rescue of the city of Halle) stunned her completely and taught her nothing. The tragedy of Mother Courage and of her life, deeply felt by the audience, consisted in the fact that here a terrible contradiction existed which destroyed a human being, a contradiction which could be resolved, but only by society itself and in long, terrible struggles. And the moral superiority of this type of presentation consisted in its showing man—even the most vigorous type of man—as destructible!

II

Notes to *Mother Courage*

The first performance of *Mother Courage and Her Children* in Zürich during the Hitler war, with the extraordinary Therese

Giehse in the title role, made it possible—in spite of the anti-
Fascist and pacifist attitude of the Zürich theatre audience, consisting mainly of German émigrés—for the bourgeois press to
speak of a "Niobe tragedy" and of the mother-animal's tremen-
dously moving energy of life. Warned by this, the playwright
made a few changes for the Berlin performance.

In the Peasants' Wars, the greatest misfortune of German history—from a sociological standpoint—the Reformation had its
canine teeth pulled. There remained: business and cynicism.
Mother Courage—let this be said by way of help to the theatrical performance—together with her friends and guests and nearly
everybody else, recognizes the purely mercantile character of the
war: that is exactly what attracts her. She believes in the war
to the end. It does not even dawn on her that you must have a
large pair of shears in order to get your own cut from a war.
The spectators at catastrophes expect without justification that
those concerned and hardest hit are going to learn from the experience. As long as the masses are the *object* of politics, they
can look upon what happens to them not as an experiment but
only as a destiny; they learn as little from the catastrophe as the
guinea pig in an experiment learns about biology. It is not the
business of the playwright to endow Mother Courage with final
insight—she does have some insight toward the middle of the
play, at the end of Scene Six, and then she loses it again; his
concern is, to make the spectator see.

III

Dramatic Form and Effect

The chronicle play, *Mother Courage and Her Children*—the
term "chronicle play" corresponds, as a literary type, approximately to the term "History" in the Elizabethan drama—naturally does not represent any attempt to convince anyone at all
about anything at all through the exposition of naked facts. Facts
very rarely allow themselves to be taken by surprise in a condi-

tion of nakedness, and they would seduce only a very few. It is of course necessary for chronicle plays to have a factual content, that is, to be realistic. Even the division, "objectivizing theatre opposed to psychologizing theatre," does not really help us along, since one can also devise theatre that would be objectivizing and psychologizing, by taking chiefly psychological "material" as the principal object of artistic presentation and at the same time striving for objectivity. So far as the present play is concerned, I do not believe that it leaves the spectator in a state of objectivity (that is, of dispassionately balancing "for" and "against"). On the contrary, I believe—or let us say, I hope—that the play makes him critical.

The Novel and the Film

ANDRÉ MALRAUX

The motion picture can tell a story, and in this is its power. So can the novel; and when talking pictures were invented, the silent film had already drawn heavily on the novel.

We can analyze the scenic presentation of a great novelist. Whether his aim is the narration of events, the depiction or analysis of characters, or even an interrogation into the meaning of life; whether his talent tends toward a proliferation, like that of Proust, or a crystallization, like that of Hemingway; he is obliged to recount—that is, to summarize—and to present scenically—to make present. I call a novelist's scenic presentation the instinctive or premeditated selection of the moments on which he seizes and the means which he employs to give them a particular importance.

With almost all novelists, the immediate sign of scenic presentation is the movement from narrative to dialogue.

Dialogue in the novel serves, first of all, for exposition.

This is the technique in the English novel of the end of the nineteenth century—of Conrad and Henry James. It tends to eliminate the absurdity of the omniscient novelist and replaces this convention by another. The film tries to use this sort of dialogue as little as possible, as is also true of the modern novel.

Next, dialogue serves to characterize. Stendhal thought much more about characterizing Julien Sorel through his actions than through the tone of his voice; but in the twentieth century, the problem of tone is a matter of first importance in the novel. It

"The Novel and the Film" is Part V of André Malraux, *Esquisse d'une psychologie du cinéma*, Librairie Gallimard, Paris, 1946. The essays which make up this work were written in 1939. Translated by Haskell M. Block.

has become one of the means of character expression, a part of a character's very existence. Proust, who hardly saw his characters at all, made them speak with the art of a blind man, and this suggests that many of his scenes, properly read, would be more intense on the radio, where the actor is invisible, than in the theatre. But the film, like the theatre, places less importance than the novel on tone in dialogue, because *the actor* suffices to give a character physical existence and even a degree of personality.

Finally, there is the essential dialogue: that of the "scene."

This cannot be described through generalization. It is what every great artist makes of it: suggestive, dramatic, elliptical, suddenly isolated from everything as in Dostoevsky, or connected to the entire universe as in Tolstoy. But for every great novelist it is the principal means of acting on the reader, the possibility of making a scene *present*—the third dimension.

And it is on this dialogue—whose nature and effect the film has just discovered—that the motion picture now bases part of its strength. In the most recent films, the director *moves to dialogue* after long sections of silence, exactly as a novelist moves to dialogue after long sections of narrative.

The novelist has still another great means of expression: the power to connect a decisive moment in the life of his character to the surrounding atmosphere or universe. Conrad uses it almost systematically, and Tolstoy has gained from it one of the most beautiful scenes in any novel, the night in which the wounded Prince André contemplates the clouds after Austerlitz. The Russian film used it forcefully in its great period.

Nevertheless, the novel seems to retain one advantage over the film: the possibility of moving to the *inside* of its characters. But on the one hand, the modern novel seems less and less to analyze its characters in their moments of crisis; and on the other hand, a dramatic psychology—that of Shakespeare and, in large measure, of Dostoevsky—in which secrets are suggested either by acts or by half confessions (Smerdyakov, Stavrogin), is perhaps no less artistically powerful nor less revealing than analysis. Finally, the mysterious part of any character not wholly explained, if expressed, as it can be on the screen, by the mystery of the human face, perhaps combines to give a work of art that sound of a questioning of life addressed to God, from which a few invincible reveries—such as Tolstoy's great short novels—derive their greatness.

The Responsibility of the Writer

JEAN-PAUL SARTRE

Dostoevsky has said: Every man is responsible to everyone for everything. This statement becomes truer from day to day. As national collectivism becomes more and more part of human collectivism, as every individual becomes more and more part of the national community, we may say that each one of us becomes more and more responsible, more and more widely responsible.

We held every German who did not protest against the Nazi regime responsible for that regime, and should there exist among us, or in any other nation, any form of economic or racial oppression, we hold responsible all those who do not denounce it. And in whatever part of the world an injustice may be committed, there are in these days so many means of communication and of exchanging news between nations, that we, too, begin to bear the responsibility for that injustice.

So that phrase, dear to the Americans, of one world, means many things, but among others it means that everyone is responsible for everything that goes on in the world.

I think we are all in agreement on this point. But if the shoemaker or the doctor is responsible as a man for everything that goes on in the world, this obviously doesn't mean that he is responsible in his capacity as doctor or shoemaker.

The shoemaker as a shoemaker has a limited responsibility

"La Responsabilité de L'Écrivain" is the text of a lecture by Jean-Paul Sartre presented at the Sorbonne, Paris, on the occasion of the first general meeting of UNESCO, November 1, 1946. It is reprinted in *Les Conférences de l'U.N.E.S.C.O.*, Editions de la Revue Fontaine, Paris, 1947, pp. 57-73. Translated by Betty Askwith in *Reflections of Our Age*, Columbia University Press, N.Y., 1948, pp. 67-83. Revised by the editors.

which consists in making good shoes. The doctor can, in the exercise of his profession, find occasions to throw himself whole-heartedly into the struggle in fighting against the unhealthiness of some particular district, in fighting against certain practices in factories where sanitary conditions are not maintained, but, in his capacity as a doctor, he is obviously not responsible for this or that persecution, as for example antisemitism.

Now, if the specialist as such is really not responsible for everything to everyone, what is the responsibility of those specialists whom we call writers? Is their responsibility as men reflected in its entirety in their work, or does the writer's responsibility rather function in the narrow limits of his specialty, that is to say, with regard to those special problems which are set by the art of writing?

This is the subject which we are going to consider. To avoid any confusion, we will limit discussion to the problem of prose.

There are, in fact, two ways of using words.

In one case, they are used as conventional signs, in which we move beyond the word itself towards the object which it signifies and gather words together so as to build up meanings and ideas.

On the other hand there is a way of considering words as natural objects. In this case we do not separate them from their meaning, but their meaning serves, so to speak, to quicken them, like a soul, and in this case there is no longer any question of grouping them together to form ideas, but of establishing between them relations entirely different but really no less natural.

To put it another way, there are two attitudes: prose and poetry. What we may ask of someone who uses words to name objects cannot be asked of one who uses words in another fashion, that is to say, who uses them as objects whose grouping produces certain effects, as do the colors of a painting.

We cannot reproach a poet with denying, in his capacity as a poet, his responsibility as a man. We may reproach him with being nothing but a poet, that is to say, with not having also, as a man, the sense of his responsibilities, but we cannot reproach him for not having entered as a poet into a social conflict or constructive movement.

We shall confine ourselves to the art of prose.

When the Germans had an oppressive Nazi government, it was obviously the duty of anti-Nazi Germans to protest, to denounce, and to resist, whether they were writers or not. But, in point of fact, it was impossible for them to exercise their function as writers, and they protested or denounced in other ways: they might join clandestine associations, they might commit an act of protest; if they were professors, for example, they might leave the university or resign their position as dean when a Jewish colleague had been dismissed; but, in any case, there was no question of protesting by means of writing.

So it is possible to imagine a man who belonged to clandestine organizations and who, while risking his life in a way that justified his existence, might yet have continued to write, assuming he had the time, works entirely free from any political significance.

And, inversely, under the occupation, many writers collaborated on underground magazines, and those whose resistance was limited to this work have always felt a sort of inferiority complex toward those who, on the contrary, were engaged in actual fighting; as if, in fact, it were not enough to resist on the literary plane—as if that were "mere literature."

So that there is a sort of oscillation in the concept of literature, whether in fact we conceive literature as something issuing directly from the human situation, which, in consequence, implies full human responsibility, or whether we write, as might be said, for the sake of writing. And precisely because we are not quite clear what literature is, there is a theory current among the writers themselves of the lack of responsibility of the writer. Somehow it is thought that to name a thing is to touch it lightly, touch it without doing it any harm.

Here is a glass on this table. When I name it as such, it would seem, theoretically, that the glass remains perfectly indifferent; that it is in no way transformed by the name I have just uttered; that it stays exactly as before, in the same place, and that this brief word I spoke in no way altered the situation. So that if in reality to speak does not mean changing anything, if in reality to speak is to bring together words which have no effect on situations, the writer can speak with an absolute irresponsibility. Literature, since it cannot change the glass by speaking of it, can only do one thing—try to copy it as well as possible in words, as the realistic painter copies it in colors, that is to say, try to reproduce the different sensations evoked by the glass. In that case, to speak would simply be to set up a world of meanings on the margin of action and of reality, which would reflect reality without modifying it. Literature would be, like consciousness, a by-product.

This view springs from a pernicious misconception, easily enough detected provided we go back to a direct examination of what language and prose really are; of the conscious or unconscious aims, the explicit or latent designs of a writer. This is what we shall examine first.

Prose is an attitude of mind, and in prose our glance traverses the words and moves on towards the thing signified. The word is thus a vehicle of ideas. When it has performed its function we forget it.

Each of us could perhaps expound one of Descartes' theories —for example, the famous "I think, therefore I am"—using words which would perfectly express this notion and would yet be quite different from those used by Descartes; one would, in short, be using words in the service of the idea.

We can say that every idea can be expressed in many ways, different and equivalent. Therefore let us keep in mind that language indicates an idea or an object; in other words, it reveals. Language is a human act of revelation. For me, and for others, words bring an object out of the shadow and integrate it into our general activity.

It is true that when I say, "the glass," I apparently change nothing. Actually, by naming it, I bring it out of the shadow for myself and for my neighbor, who may not have noticed it, who may have had a vague general view of this room, in which the glass passed unperceived. Thus, from this moment the glass exists

for him, and to this extent his universe is changed thereby, however trivial the change may be. There is now for him an object
which exists and which before did not exist. I named it and,
because of this, he realized that it is a component of the universe and has something to do with him.

When we remember that people have used violence and torture just to extract one word (a telephone number or an address
or a name), we understand how important the act of naming is,
and that to name a thing is to transform it.

How transform it?

First of all by removing an object from the immediate to the
mediate state in the world of human knowledge, consciousness,
and culture. All of us do many things that we should prefer to
ignore because we do not want to be responsible for them. We
do them without paying attention, we gloss over them in silence,
we go through our lives passing actions over in silence just because we do not want to name them. To pass them over in
silence means committing them without a conscious reflex, without coming back to look at them; we act, we do not watch ourselves act.

To name one of these actions is to present it, whatever it may
be, to its author, saying, "This is what you're doing now; come
to grips with it." The deed, thus named, loses its innocence. In
some sort of way, language does away with innocence. Language
removes immediacy and at the same time brings the person face
to face with his responsibilities.

The oppression of Negroes is nothing, so long as no one says,
"Negroes are oppressed." Until then, nobody realizes it, perhaps
not even the Negroes themselves; but it only needs a word for
the act to take on a meaning.

From the moment in which I give a name to my neighbor's
conduct, he knows what he does. In addition, he knows that I
know it, and in consequence his attitude towards me is changed.
He knows that others know it or could know it, and his conduct
moves out of the subjective and becomes part of the objective
mind.

Literature, therefore, precisely because it is prose and it gives names to objects, consists in moving immediate, unreflected, perhaps ignored events on to the plane of reflection and of the objective mind.

In speaking, I know I make a change. It is not possible for me to speak if it is not in order to make a change, unless I am talking just for the sake of talking; but to talk is to make a change and to be conscious of making it.

You know that beautiful and wonderfully significant remark in Stendhal's *Chartreuse de Parme?* La Sanseverina and Fabrice have a vague feeling for each other which causes Count Mosca much anxiety. Watching the carriage in which they are traveling, he exclaims, "If the word love passes between them, I am lost." This means that if the thing be once named it is done. The name is enough.

Well, the writer, *whether he wishes it or not,* is a man who gives the names of love and hate to undefinable relationships between men, who gives to social relationships the names of oppression and fellowship. I say: whether he wishes it or not, since he can, obviously, choose not to speak of them, but silence is also a word since when one is concerned with the world of language, silence defines itself in relation to words. Silence is a sort of cement between words, and it *means* something. To be silent is yet to speak; one does not say of a dumb man that he is silent.

If therefore a writer has chosen to be silent on one aspect of the world, we have the right to ask him: why have you spoken of this rather than that? And since you speak in order to make a change, since there is no other way you can speak, why do you want to change this rather than that? Why do you want to alter the way in which postage stamps are made rather than the way in which Jews are treated in an antisemitic country? And the other way around. He must therefore always answer the following questions: What do you want to change? Why this rather than that?

Thus we may ask the writer: Why do you want to speak, and of what, on the whole, do you want to speak?

But, moreover, the writer is one who uses language by grouping words in a way he hopes will be attractive. Why does he do this? I think a writer speaks in order to be recognized by others, in the sense in which Hegel speaks of human consciousnesses recognizing one another.

I think we have badly misunderstood what the aesthetic presentation of a thing means. It is true that aesthetic values always indicate a presentation at a certain distance, the object is moved back in relation to the spectator. There is no monster, said Boileau, which does not become agreeable if it is imitated by art. This means that if the artist shows a wound, or something ugly, or an act of injustice, in a work of art, he does not aim at appealing to the spectator directly, physically, as, for instance, one might do if he needed help or money. Thus a belief has arisen that aesthetic presentation means pure presentation, presentation without commitment, enabling the writer to escape into irresponsibility.

Let us try to understand what aesthetic pleasure means and we shall perhaps understand what this presentation means. The writer wants his work to be recognized not as a cry rising from his animal self, under the impact of pain, bewilderment, or fear, but as the result of a planned creation, that is to say, doubly free; free first of all as a creation, since, by its very definition, if we create something it means that the germ of that thing was not wholly contained in the preceding moment. If we create, it means that there is something new in relation to any anticipation that might have been made at the immediately preceding moment. Free, secondly, in the sense of planned, that is to say, as an activity which regulates itself by its own laws. Here we find the second sense of freedom, autonomy, the possibility of acting by the representation of laws and not under the stress of laws. Consequently, this double character implies that the author, when he has taken pains to invent something and create it according to a plan, demands that he be recognized as free because he is the author of a free creation.

The reader on the other hand, does not bring to the book or to the work of art a judgment of fact but a judgment of value. It is customary for a hostess, when she sees that a discussion of a particular book or play threatens to become heated, to remind people that all this is a matter of taste, and it is polite to say: "I like" or "I don't like such a book," because it is understood that you don't like it in the same way that you may dislike shrimps or tomatoes; but not to say, "This book is good" or "This book is bad."

We have recourse to this evasion for a very simple reason. If you say, "This book is good," that means, "I hold people guilty who do not think that it is good"; or if you prefer, "I insist that everybody in the community to which I belong shall recognize this book as good." It is this insistence which offends people. But insistence on whatever it may be always postulates the freedom of the person to whom it is addressed. You must, therefore you can. I absolutely cannot insist on a person's making an aesthetic judgment if he is not free: he would be the slave of his taste. And I myself—at the moment when I insist that a person by stating the simple formula, "This book is good," asserts as I do the merits of this book—I declare at the same time, as I have told you, that I am in the presence of a planned creation, and that at the same time an appeal is being made to my freedom.

An appeal is made to my freedom because I am asked to make a universal judgment: "This is good." No attempt, therefore, is made to arouse me on the individual plane, on the plane of my passions, of my complexes; I am at once asked to put myself on the plane of universality. Hence, I am addressed insofar as I am a free person, and that is the meaning of the aesthetic perspective. It is not that I am not meant to be indignant over injustice, it is not that things are presented to my impartial self; no: it is hoped that my judgment will be involved, but it must be freely involved. This appeal is not made to the flesh, but to what is truly human in man, to his liberty.

Aesthetic judgment, then, is the recognition that I am face to face with a certain form of freedom, the freedom of the creator; secondly, and simultaneously, the recognition of the consciousness, in virtue of the object confronting me, of my own freedom; and, lastly, an insistence that other men in the same circumstances should enjoy the same freedom.

Thus, as you see, a book conceived on the aesthetic plane is really a summons by one freedom to another, and aesthetic pleasure is an active awareness of freedom concerning its object.

And since literature is a perpetual affirmation of human freedom, since in its quest for beauty it constantly invokes that freedom, it is false to say that there is such a thing as pessimistic literature. There is only good and bad literature. If literature is good it is never pessimistic, because, apart from any subject it may treat, it invites its readers to place themselves on a plane on which they are free and on which, therefore, they can *change* what they are shown: in themselves, if it is a description of psychological and subjective outrages; in the world, if they are presented with social injustice.

Thus the writer is a man who appeals to the freedom of others so that this freedom may recognize its own. And as liberty does not contemplate itself but fulfills itself, he makes this appeal in view of something which he wants to change.

If for a moment we compare the writer to the politician, we see that the politician may put before himself the aim of achieving freedom; but that he has no other means of achieving it except through violence. The violence may be reduced to a minimum, but it cannot be suppressed altogether, since it must at least be used against those who seek to do away with the freedom which he wants to secure for everyone. It is the famous question: Should a democracy allow the enemies of democracy to exist? The writer, on the contrary, finds himself in a position where, aiming at freedom like the politician, wanting to achieve the kingdom of man, like the politician, he has no need to commit violence. He rejects violence.

There is a possible violence of words which consists in lying, in suppressing, in dissimulating. But then, we are no longer on the plane of literature, we are on the plane of propaganda or of advertisement. If we really want our work to be good we aim precisely at making an appeal, without violence, to freedom.

Thus we can, at this stage, define in broad terms the responsibility of the writer.

If the writer is a maker of literature; in other words, if he writes—it is because he is assuming the function of perpetuating, in a world where freedom is always threatened, the assertion of freedom and the appeal to freedom.

A writer who does not take his stand on this ground is guilty; not only is he guilty, but he soon ceases to be a writer.

One of the most curious things which could be noticed during the occupation was the growing uneasiness of Drieu la Rochelle. Drieu la Rochelle, who was certainly one of the sincerest and perhaps one of the most pathetic among those who deceived themselves, had a literary review in which he regularly insulted muzzled men, men who could not answer back, who were not free. Well, this man, who was not without insight, gradually became disturbed, and this showed in his writings; anger gave way to uneasiness, and finally he abandoned his review, just because he was speaking to people who could not answer back, just because he was speaking to people who were not free to pass judgment on what he wrote. His voice fell silent just because of that. You cannot write, you cannot speak in a desert.

Thus, since this is what the writer wants, we shall say that he is once and for all responsible for human freedom. But here we come up against far more concrete and far more difficult problems. Should he, in this case, be a scholar like the late Monsieur Benda, and without entering the battle, since the battle is always unjust, ponder over the ideas of eternal good, of eternal justice, of the true, the truth, and the eternal. Does he betray his vocation if the speaks of Nazis, of Spain, of the Resistance in oppressed nations, of the Jewish question, of the proletariat, of the coming war? Is he merely the custodian of eternal values? The answer must be: No. We are not custodians of eternal values, for freedom is concrete.

When I say that a book is an appeal to freedom, I am not talking about an appeal to an abstract freedom which would simply be a sort of metaphysical function of mankind. Of this we know nothing except in philosophical treatises; but nobody adopts a course of action with a view to maintaining an absolute, eternal, merely abstract liberty.

When we fight for something, there is a way of wanting that thing which is a way of implicitly wanting freedom. We may be fighting only to raise the intellectual level of a certain group, to lay claim on behalf of these people or on behalf of others to some definite rights, and it is in doing this that we perpetuate and assert human freedom.

On the other hand, if we limit ourselves to writing on freedom in general, we contribute simply, as I shall soon point out, to oppression, since total oppression is possible in the name of freedom.

Freedom is made day by day and concretely in concrete actions in which it is implicit, and therefore, when we speak of an involvement of the writer, of a responsibility of the writer, it does not mean involvement in the name of an abstract freedom. The freedom to which the writer appeals when he writes is a concrete freedom that realizes its function in something concrete. It is a concrete indignation concerning a particular event, it is to a will to change a particular institution that he appeals.

In order fully to understand what I have been saying, we must enter into certain historical considerations, because, fundamentally, apart from what I have just said to you, that is, that the essence of literature is the maintenance of freedom, there is no *a priori* problem of the writer's responsibility; it changes with the times. Indeed, it is not only the writer who is responsible to the extent of his responsibility; it is also the society in which he moves. A writer of the eighteenth century or the fifteenth century was not responsible in the same way as is a writer of the twentieth century. There was one period, the Middle Ages, in which the writer could in fact contemplate eternal good or could have the illusion of contemplating it.

Why? Because there was little solidarity among social groups; because it was easy to picture a small community living in a relatively isolated manner, and, in consequence, a band of scholars; because books were little read, except by an elite, and that elite possessed a ready-made ideology, the Christian ideology, and because beyond all this there was a fixed power, the Church or the State, which maintained this ideology.

The stronger the ideology held by the ruling classes, the less the writer who is always in touch with the governing classes is responsible, the more he inclines to be merely the guardian of that ideology, and as it always claims to be eternal, it is obvious that he is going to be an observer of eternal values.

Therefore the writer at certain periods such as those I have mentioned limited himself, on the surface, to establishing the values and ideology of the classes in power at the moment. And yet he went beyond them as a writer, because, nevertheless, he placed them face to face with freedom. His work was a constant appeal to human liberty because without even realizing it himself, implicitly, by the mere fact of presenting these values, by dint of holding them up to observation and discussion, by dint of naming them, he invited men to go beyond them. To speak of an ideology as of a given thing is already to go beyond it in part.

There are certain types of periods, for example the eighteenth century, in which we find an ideological liquidation, in which one class is about to replace another, in which an ideology liquidates itself through criticism.

In such times the writer is bound up with the movement of History. His task of presentation, of criticism, of placing ideologies face to face with freedom, goes hand in hand with the critical effort occurring at the heart of society, as the result of a displacement of classes.

You all know what responsibilities the writers of the eighteenth century had, such as Rousseau, such as Voltaire. But theirs was an age of liquidation.

The nineteenth century, on the other hand, marked the end of the revolutionary apocalypse, the birth of a new ideology, the liberal ideology: political rights for all, the existence of an elite founded on work, progress, and frugality. At this time, instead of falling into line with a class whose ideology was firm and stable as in the Middle Ages, instead of aligning himself with a rising class, engaged in liquidating the ideology of those who were once oppressed, the writer was out of harmony with the class which produced him, he was in opposition to that ideology. At the same time, he had no grip on the proletariat or else he ignored it and, unable to furnish his own class with ideas, which had a stable and ready-made ideology, he was relegated to the contemplation of pure values, that is to say, to a sterile appeal to freedom.

To appeal to freedom without a desire to change anything, only in order that liberty may take its pleasure in the presence of a beautiful work of art, is what is known as creating art for art's sake. This way of appealing to creative freedom against the useful, against mechanical progress, against classes, is a way of being at one and the same time against the bourgeoisie and materially attached to the bourgeoisie.

The bourgeoisie is delighted to pay a writer to vent his anger against its philistinism, its lack of taste and intelligence, when such wrath might have been directed on oppression, which would be far more inconvenient.

Thus, art for art's sake derives from the comfortable observation that the writer, not being in harmony with his own class, or indeed with any other, cannot help anyone.

Hence, the theory that the writer is irresponsible, that is to say, free solely to create, and to create in innocence.

As I have said, there is no innocent literature; in the same way as Saint-Just declared, one cannot govern in innocence, so we must say, one cannot speak, one cannot write in innocence. Writers are guilty of having maintained too long the doctrine of art for art's sake.

Today the situation is altogether different because, first of all, no one believes any more in irresponsibility or in art for art's sake. The Occupation, for instance, showed many people that literature today is bound up with democracy. If you cannot write freely by addressing yourself to free men, you cannot write at all.

The example of Drieu, of which I spoke, as also that of the Resistance writers, shows that literature is so closely allied to democracy at this point that not only must democracy defend it, but, when democracy is attacked by armed violence, literature must also be defended by armed violence.

Thus, as you see, the writer's position calls for a particular human society. It cannot exist in all societies; in an oppressed society literature ceases to exist, and it was not due to chance that Nazi German literature or Fascist Italian literature was so bad.

Secondly, there is an infinite widening of the public—but on the surface, as you shall see.

I said just now, one world; that is why today we are witnessing a strange phenomenon, which is that writers who do not yet deserve and perhaps never will deserve, their reputation, writers, such as myself and many others of my generation, have already a public greater than writers of the first rank had, for example, in the nineteenth century. One blushes at being translated and read abroad when he thinks of the tiny circle which recognized Baudelaire during his lifetime. But this is a phenomenon which means no more than this, that there are newspapers, radios, the movies; yet at the same time, while enlarging the writer's public, it places on him much more responsibility in the sense that he has to know many more things and to speak of many more things.

The writer of today, however, still comes from the bourgeois class or, in any case, is read by the bourgeois class. If the words "bourgeois class" jar on you because they have a political tone, let us say, if you prefer, that the writer is read by the governing social group, by professional men, by what we call the enlightened few. He speaks to doctors, to lawyers, civil servants, teachers. But these social groups are witnessing today the liquidation of their ideology. We have to deal with a paradoxical situation. In the eighteenth century the writer wrote for a rising class, which itself criticized abuses and prejudices. In the nineteenth century the writer found himself shut out both from a proletariat of which he knew nothing and from a middle class rooted in a very stable ideology, which asked nothing of him except to provide it with beauty.

Today, those who come to the writer, who write every day to all the writers in the world to ask for advice, for help, for an ideology, are still the bourgeois, bourgeois of good will, intellectuals, professional men, who are witnessing the liquidation of bourgeois ideology, who know that liberalism has had its day, who see the doctrine of *laissez-faire* replaced everywhere by planning, and individualism by national intervention, who have no longer the same peace of mind about their property, and, moreover, who have often lost the greater part of what they owned.

These people, who mean well, come to the writers, but they are still bourgeois. They make up the writer's public and place him, whether he wishes it or not, under the obligation of remaking an ideology for a class which, while still in control, is in process of liquidating itself.

On the other hand, he seldom reaches, perhaps less than ever today, the most important part of all national communities, the peasants and the workers. He cannot reach them for the same reasons which prevented him from reaching the nineteenth-century bourgeoisie; he cannot reach them because the most active, the most enlightened among them already have a ready-made ideology. The worker's society is organized as a closed society, it has an ideology of struggle: determinism, materialism.

The writer, to the extent that he postulates and demands freedom, cannot furnish the governing class, nor any other class, with an ideology, except one which insists on the freedom of men who still remain oppressed. And, on the other hand, he cannot address himself to those whose freedom he desires, unless he becomes a member of a party and acts as a member of that party by becoming a propagandist, by allowing his art to become propaganda; that is, by calling for the death of literature and ceasing to be a writer.

Thus, it is not possible that the writer should accept the position of speaking only to the bourgeoisie. He must speak of others, he must speak *for* them and he must speak *to* them. But he cannot. He is responsible insofar as he is a writer, because he must demand their liberation; he feels himself guilty as a member issuing from or attached to the oppressing classes, and yet he has no other audience than the men of good will in the class which is in the process of disappearing, which still governs and begins to be conscious of being an oppressing class. Those to whom he wants most urgently to speak will not listen to him.

If we wish to discover what he should speak about today, the

179

matter becomes even more complicated. He springs from the class which made the Revolution of 1789. He remains attached to it whether he likes it or not, since one does not cease to be a bourgeois just by wishing, and he reflects the principles which lay at the origin of the apocalypse of freedom, that is to say, the principles of '89: *habeas corpus*, freedom of thought, political freedom. But he realizes at the same time that these principles are no more than pure and simple mystification for millions of people. Mystification for the Louisiana Negro; mystification for the worker in a factory at Melun; it is nothing but mystification to speak of such principles to them. There must be, he knows, a more complete liberation on the economic and social plane for the principles of *habeas corpus*, political freedom, and freedom of thought to take on meaning again. Thus, when a writer tries to defend freedom of thought, although he is perfectly right, he feels that he does it with a bad conscience, because in one way, it is only his own freedom that he is defending. What does freedom of thought mean to a worker in a shoe factory? Thus, in the first place there is this obligation: that he must denounce, in the name of certain democratic principles, a certain type of abuse. But, at the same time, he realizes that there must be a deeper liberation. Now, I have told you that those who desire this deeper liberation have no audience unless they join the Communist Party. Moreover, the necessities of action have forced a segment of these working-class organizations to assert the primacy of Machiavellianism over morality, of violence, of opportunism, and in a general way, the doctrine that the end justifies the means.

They have been led to this, not through the ill will of this or that individual, but because war and violence inevitably leads men, at a certain stage, to these principles; for there is an end to be attained, which is the total freedom of mankind, and this freedom will not be brought about by making poems or by all men one fine day suddenly embracing one another. Thus we have a struggle, a war; and the necessity of war demands the primacy of Machiavellianism. It is quite obvious that it is not by simply preaching morality that one always gets things done. But the unhappy writer finds himself in a deeply contradictory and paradoxical situation. He is in agreement about the end with these organizations we spoke about, completely in agreement; he must be, because he insists on freedom. But he is in agreement with the bourgeoisie, who brought him up, who taught him his principles, which incidentally are also principles of freedom, in condemning the unconditional use of means to an end. He asserts, by the very fact that he writes, the primacy of morality; he declares that there is a primacy of moral values higher than any Machiavellianism. Yet, in the name of ethical values, he must demand plainly and above all else—for otherwise he is an oppressor or a trickster—the liberation of all oppressed people, proletarians, Jews, Negroes, colonial subjects, occupied countries, and so on.

If he demands this concretely, if it is not merely a matter of words, how does he think it will be possible to liberate an occupied country, how does he think one can set about freeing the Negroes, or the subject peoples of colonies? To achieve this one must resort to action, and doubtless to violence, and in consequence, fall once more into the Machiavellianism which he condemns.

If, on the other hand, he limits himself to condemning Machiavellianism, merely declaring that the oppressed must be set free, without adding anything more, then either he is speaking in the air and is simply a passionate idealist, or else it is a dodge which consists, so to speak, in "drowning the fish." He is wrong either way. He swings from side to side without a pause. This is the situation of most of our writers today; now sickened by Machiavellianism, they condemn it whatever it is, forgetting the end which in a certain sense justifies it, and thus they swing back to make-believe out of their insufficiency. They again condemn a certain act in the name of *habeas corpus,* without realizing that *habeas corpus* has no relevance to the present day; that the problem is much deeper, much more complex. Or else, hypnotized by the end in view, convinced that everything must be done that can set men free, they become remorseful, take on inferiority complexes and blindly accept the *means,* without the ability to judge them. The result is that they contribute to the liquidation of moral values; they come to justify Machiavellianism still more thoroughly. In the end they even cease to be writers; if they are poets, they will cease being poets and will end up by going into advertising.

We have all helped to do away with moral values, all of us writers have contributed to the assertion that Machiavellianism rules the day, because we have an inferiority complex about the end, because we hesitate between an individualistic morality of the eighteenth century and a social morality, because we are forced to choose between the end and the means.

Or else we keep quiet. Today in many countries, particularly in France, there is a conspiracy of silence. Writers are constantly haunted by qualms of conscience about the means or about the ends, with the result that we are always keeping something back. There are writers who, for fear of Soviet Russia—that is to say, for fear of the means—will refuse to condemn certain unseemly activities and certain policies, such as, for example, Great Britain's policy in Greece or Palestine. And on the other hand there are writers who, because they are anti-capitalist, and because they care primarily for the end, will keep quiet about a certain number of deportations carried out by Soviet Russia, or about the way in which Russia handles elections in certain occupied countries.

Therefore there is silence among us, because it seems that everything cannot be denounced at once. There is silence about war. There are writers who think that America is preparing for war, but as they would be very happy about a preventive war in the name of *habeas corpus*, they are silent about this preparation. There are writers who think that Russia is preparing for war, but as, after all, war will perhaps pave the way for revolution, they too are silent. I have no idea if these two countries are preparing for war, but they certainly would be able to do so quite easily. No one today will raise his voice to say that they should not.

Thus the writer finds himself in a curious situation; he is invested with a responsibility which he does not know what to do with, and faced by the most drastic problems that have ever perhaps been presented to mankind. I hasten to add—I don't want to make him out too interesting—that in this he is exactly like everyone else, only it happens that since he has chosen to speak he must speak of all this, and what is he to say about it?

I think that here, too, there is a formal attitude which is more or less clear. It is clear that in the name of freedom the writer must condemn injustice, that is to say, evil, wherever it comes from. He must condemn violence. He must condemn no matter what violence, whether it be violence employed by his friends or by his enemies, whether it be violence employed in order to preserve a certain democracy according to the principles of the eighteenth century. But if he does only this, he will always end by condemning the violent acts of the working class and of Soviet Russia more than any other, because he will be placed in a position in which he forgets the end and is concerned only with the means.

We must know on what principle violence is condemned. We must begin by realizing that we live in a violent universe, that violence was not invented by those who are now using it, that everything is violence. But under these conditions the writer must try to construct for himself a theory of violence, he must understand that there are many kinds of violence, that there is violence to fight violence.

It is possible that there are a million deported persons in certain countries occupied by the Russians. Very well. I am told: "We must protest vigorously against this." On the other hand, people say to me: "It is too bad that a Negro should have been lynched—in Alabama, for example. But it is only one Negro. Here we have one, and there, one million."

First of all, I should say that from a strictly ethical standpoint, there is absolutely no reason for making a distinction between one person and one million, but I think that is a little academic.

Let us look at it another way. In the first instance, if this deportation took place it strongly deserves condemnation, but it is a means for arriving at an end. I don't say that excuses it, but it must be considered from this angle. On the other hand, the lynching of the Negro is an effect of a situation which goes on of its own accord; it is in no way a means to an end, it is an act of pure violence, and it is only the expression of a situation which is that of ten million Negroes, which has been that of ten million Negroes before them, and which will be that, perhaps, of ten million Negroes after them. In other words, we find ourselves in this situation, in the midst of a tradition of oppression. In the two cases, the oppression does not always spring from the same causes.

I don't wish to defend one point of view against another. I merely want to say that a writer must not condemn violence *a priori;* he must condemn it within its setting while looking on it as a means; and above all, he must understand that he will do well to try not to condemn violence in general and in the abstract, but to try to determine in each case the minimum of necessary violence. Because, today, nothing can be done without violence, because everything is violence. The question is, therefore, not to condemn all violence, but only to condemn useless violence.

Otherwise stated, the problem which the writer has to solve for himself and to make clear to others is the problem of the relation of ends and means. It is a vital problem, and our responsibility as a writer is to try to clear it up.

This leads you on, obviously, if you say to yourself: "But I do not condemn violence unconditionally, I condemn violence when it is not for a certain end and when it is not the minimum necessary to arrive at that end." This leads you on, inevitably, as a writer, to raise the problem of the end in view.

There is no question of a writer's condemning a theory, an action or a practice, from a purely negative standpoint. He must necessarily condemn in the name of something. Thus we must again think out the problem of liberation and of freedom. We must realize that if *habeas corpus* is bewildering today, it is because of a deeper freedom; it is this freedom which we must try to understand, to attain, and to achieve.

There is a new freedom to be achieved; therefore we must think about it in a new way. If we are to condemn Machiavellianism, it cannot be done in the name of a freedom which millions do not possess, it must be in the name of an end which excludes Machiavellianism, and which we must define. In other words, I do not think it possible for a contemporary writer to have a clear conscience as a writer, if he has not defined the socialism which will provide concrete and positive freedom, if he is not thinking precisely on this plane, if he has not defined it concretely and for himself as well, or if—for after all, it is no easy task—he has not at least tried to do it, if he has not contributed toward doing it.

Thus the responsibility of the writer, today, is very clear:

He must construct a positive theory of liberation and freedom.

He must put himself in every instance in the position of condemning violence from the point of view of the members of the oppressed classes.

And he must establish a true relationship between ends and means.

He must refuse forthwith, in the name of freedom— which will not, of course, prevent anything—to sanction any means of violence to establish or sustain an order.

He must, finally, give his thoughts without respite, day in, day out, to the problem of the end and the means; or, again, the problem of the relationship of ethics and politics.

This is our problem; it is the problem of the present age, and it is our own problem, it belongs to us, writers. That is our responsibility, not eternal but contemporary.

If the writer deals with the problem of good or evil in the abstract, then he betrays his trust, for this is not what men ask of him. Everybody knows what good is in the abstract; what is required of him is to try to help men of good will to think out these problems. His success is altogether another matter, and besides, I have not been asked to talk to you on that topic. In any case, it is certain that a European writer who belongs to a country which is either definitely incapable of taking its place again in the world order, or else is incapable of this for the time being, cannot hope that his ideas, whatever they may be, will, solely through his own efforts, reach the masses of the one side and the other, the masses of those countries which at present have a special importance in History. Thus, what is needed is a relay network; that is to say, he must aim not only at influencing the readers in his own country, but also the writers in foreign countries, who will serve him as relays, as he will serve them in the same way, so as to gain expression for his protests, his definitions.

This is why a body like UNESCO is necessary.

In the end, after he has tried to do all that I have described, it is possible that it will have served no purpose. It is possible that the war which we are trying to avoid will come. It is possible that he will not reach anyone. What we must avoid, we writers, is that our responsibility change into guilt, so that in fifty years it may be said of us: "They saw the greatest world catastrophe coming and they kept silent."

We Write for Our Own Time

JEAN-PAUL SARTRE

We take our stand against certain critics and authors. We declare that salvation must be won upon this earth, that it must be won for the whole man by the whole man, and that art is a meditation on life, not on death. It is true that, for history, only talent is important. But I have not yet entered history, and I do not know how I will enter it: perhaps alone, perhaps in an anonymous crowd, perhaps as one of those names that one finds in the notes of textbooks on literature. In any case, I shall not worry about the judgments that the future may pronounce upon my work, because there is nothing I can do about them. Art cannot be reduced to a dialogue with dead men and men as yet unborn: that would be both too hard and too easy. In my opinion, this idea constitutes the last trace of the Christian belief in immortality: just as the sojourn of man upon this earth is represented as a brief testing time between Limbo and Hell or Heaven, so a book is supposed to enjoy a transitory period that is approximately the same as that of its effectiveness; after that, disincarnated and free as a soul, it enters eternity. But at least for Christians our sojourn upon earth is the decisive factor and eternal beatitude is only a reward. Yet people seem to believe that the career our books have after we are no more should be justified by the life we once led. This is true from an objective point of view. Objectively, we are classified according to our talent. But the perspective our grandchildren will have upon us

"Ecrire pour son époque" was first published in *Valeurs* (Alexandria), No. 7-8, January 1947, and is reprinted in *Les Temps Modernes*, t. III (June 1948), pp. 2113-2121. The translation, by Sylvia Glass, "We Write for Our Own Time," appears in *The Virginia Quarterly Review*, Vol. XXIII (Spring, 1947), pp. 236-243.

is not infallible, since others will come after them and judge them in their turn. It goes without saying that we all write out of need for the absolute; and a work of the spirit is, indeed, an absolute. However, people make a double mistake on this score. First, it is not true that a writer raises his sufferings or his errors to the level of the absolute by writing about them; and it is not true that he redeems them. People say of the unhappily married man who writes well about marriage that he has made a good book *out* of his conjugal misery. That would be too easy. The bee makes honey *out of* the flower by causing *real* transformations in the substance of the flower; the sculptor makes a statue *out* of marble. But the writer makes books out of words, not out of his sorrows. If he wants to stop his wife from behaving badly, he should not write about her; he should beat her. One cannot *put* one's misfortunes into a book, any more than one can put a model on a canvas; one draws inspiration from one's misfortunes—and they remain as they are. Perhaps one gets temporary consolation from placing oneself above them in order to describe them, but once the book is finished, one finds them again. Bad faith begins when the artist tries to give meaning, a sort of immanent finality, to his troubles and persuades himself that they are there *so that* he can talk about them. When he justifies his own sufferings by this deception, he makes himself ridiculous; but he is despicable if he tries to justify the sufferings of others in the same fashion. The most beautiful book in the world will not redeem the sufferings of a child. We cannot redeem evil, we must combat it. The most beautiful book in the world redeems itself and redeems the artist, but not the man; no more than the man can redeem the artist. We want the man and the artist to win salvation together; we want the work of art to be an act as well; we want it to be expressly conceived as a weapon in man's struggle against evil.

The other mistake is equally serious: there is in every human heart such a hunger for the absolute that people have often confused eternity, which would be a timeless absolute, with immortality, which is only a perpetual delay of execution and a long series of vicissitudes. I understand this desire for the absolute very well. I desire it also. But need we go so far afield to look for it? It is there all around us, under our feet and in all our gestures. We make absolutes, just as M. Jourdain made prose. You light your pipe and that is an absolute; you don't like oysters and that is an absolute; you join the Communist Party and that is an absolute. Whether the world is matter or spirit, whether God exists or does not exist, whether the judgment of future centuries is favorable or hostile to you, nothing will ever be able to negate the fact that you passionately loved such and such a picture, such and such a cause, and such and such a woman; that you lived that love from day to day: lived it, willed it, and undertook it; and that you engaged your whole being in it. Our grandfathers were perfectly right when they used to say as they drank their glass of wine: "One more that the Prussians won't have." Neither the Prussians nor anyone else. People may kill you or deprive you of wine for the rest of your life; but that last drop of Bordeaux that slipped over your palate, no God and no man can take it away from you. Not relativity; nor the "eternal course of history"; nor the dialectic of perception; nor the dissociations of psychoanalysis. That drop of wine is a pure event and we, too, in the very depths of historical relativity and our own insignificance, are absolutes, inimitable and incomparable, and our choice of ourselves is an absolute. All the vital and passionate choices that we are and that we are perpetually making with or against other people, all the common undertakings into which we throw ourselves from birth until death, all the bonds of love and hate that unite us with each other and that exist only in so far as we feel them, the enormous complexes of movements that supplement or negate each other and that are lived, this whole discordant and harmonious life combines to create a new absolute which I like to call the *time*. The time is intersubjectivity, the living absolute, the dialectical other side of history. It is born in the pangs of events that historians will later stick labels on. Blindly, in fury, in fear, and in enthusiasm, it lives the meanings that they will later define by rational methods. In its own time, each word, before it is an historical slogan or the recognizable origin of a social process,

189

is first an insult or a call or a confession. Economic phenomena themselves, before they are the theoretical causes of social up-heavals, are suffered in humiliation or despair. Ideas are tools or flights; facts are born of intersubjectivity and unsettle it as emotions unsettle the individual soul. Men make history out of dead times, because each time, upon its death, enters into rela-tivity and takes its place in the line of the centuries with the other dead. Then people try to throw new light upon it, dispute its meaning with their new knowledge, resolve its problems, prove that its most ardent searchings were doomed to failure, that the great undertakings of which it was most proud had opposite results to those it hoped for; suddenly its limitations appear and its ignorance. But all this is *because that time is dead;* those limits and that ignorance did not exist "at the time": men do not live a lack; or rather, that time was a perpetual over-stepping of its own limits toward a future which was *its* future and which is dead with it. It was *that* boldness, *that* imprudence, *that* ignorance of its own ignorance: to live means to make short-term provisions and to manage on one's margin. Perhaps our fathers, had they had a little more knowledge, would have under-stood that such and such a problem was insoluble and that such and such a question should not have been raised in those terms. But the human condition requires that we make our choice in ignorance; it is ignorance that makes morality possible. If we knew all the factors that condition events, if we could play our hand without uncertainty, risk would disappear; and with risk, courage and fear, waiting, the final joy, and effort; we would be languid Gods, but certainly not men. The bitter quarrels of the Babylonians over the meaning of omens, the bloody and passionate heresies of the Albigensians and the Anabaptists to-day seem to us errors. At the time, men were completely in them, and by asserting them at the price of their lives, gave rise to truth indirectly, for truth never yields itself directly; it makes its appearance only in combination with errors. The fate of human Reason was at stake in the quarrel of the Universals and in that of the Immaculate Conception or Transubstantiation. And at the time of the great lawsuits of certain American states against the teachers who taught the theory of evolution, it was again the fate of Reason that was at stake. It is absolutely at stake in every period in connection with doctrines that the next period will condemn as false. It is possible that some day the belief in evolution will seem the greatest folly of our century: yet, in supporting it against the churchmen, the American teachers *lived* the truth, they lived it passionately and absolutely at great risk to themselves. Tomorrow they will be wrong, today they are absolutely right: the time is always wrong when it is dead, always right when it is alive. Let people condemn it after the fact, if they wish; nevertheless, it had its own passionate way of loving itself and tearing itself apart, against which future judgments will be of no avail; it had its own taste which it alone tasted and which was as incomparable, as irremediable as the taste of wine in our mouth.

A book has its absolute truth in its own time. It is lived like a riot or a famine, with much less intensity, of course, and by fewer people, but in the same way. It is an emanation of inter-subjectivity, a living bond of rage, hatred, or love between those who have produced it and those who receive it. If it gains ground, thosuands of people reject it and deny it: we all know very well that to read a book is to rewrite it. *At the time* it is first a panic, an escape, or a courageous affirmation; at the time it is a good or a bad *action*. Later, when the time has died, it will become relative; it will become a message. But the judgment of posterity will not invalidate the opinions men had of it during its lifetime. People have often said to me about dates and bananas, "You can't judge them: to know what they are really like, you have to eat them on the spot, just after they have been picked." And I have always considered bananas a dead fruit whose real taste escaped me. The books which pass from one period to another are dead fruits, too. We should have read *Emile* or *The Persian Letters* just after they were picked.

Thus we must write for our time, as the great writers did. But this does not imply that we must shut ourselves up in it. To write for our time does not mean to reflect it passively. It means that we must will to maintain it or change it; therefore, go beyond it toward the future; and it is this effort to change it which establishes us most deeply in it, for it can never be reduced to a dead mass of tools and customs. It is in flux, it perpetually goes beyond itself; in it the concrete present and the living future of all the men who compose it exactly coincide. If, among other characteristics, Newtonian physics and the theory of the noble savage help to define the first half of the eighteenth century, we must not forget that the former represented a consistent effort to wrest fragments of the truth from the fog of ignorance in order to reach, beyond the contemporary state of knowledge, an ideal science in which phenomena could be deduced mathematically from the principle of gravitation, and that the latter was an attempt to go beyond the vices of civilization and restore the state of nature. Both theories outlined a future; and if it is true that this future never became a present, that men later renounced the Golden Age and the idea of making science a strictly logical chain of reasons, it is nonetheless true that these profound and vital hopes sketched a future beyond men's daily cares and that in order to penetrate the meaning of our day-to-day existence we must approach it with the future *as our point of departure*. One cannot be a man or make oneself a writer without drawing a line on the horizon beyond oneself, but this going beyond oneself is in each case finite and unique. One does not go beyond *in general* and for the simple pride and pleasure of going beyond. Baudelairian dissatisfaction represents only the abstract scheme of transcendence and, since it is a dissatisfaction with everything, ends by being a dissatisfaction with nothing. Real transcendence requires that one wish to change certain definite aspects of the world and any going beyond is colored by and characterized by the concrete situation it seeks to modify. A man throws himself completely into his plan for freeing the Negroes or restoring the Hebrew language to the Jews of Palestine; he throws himself into it completely and at the same time expresses man's fate in all its universality, but it must always be through a unique and dated undertaking. And if people say to me, as does Monsieur Jean Schlumberger, that one also goes beyond one's time when one strives for immortality,

I shall answer that this is a false going beyond: instead of wishing to change an intolerable situation, one attempts to escape from it and seeks refuge in a future that is entirely strange to us, since it is not the future that we *make*, but the concrete present of our grandchildren. We have no way of affecting that present; they will live it for themselves and as they wish, situated in their own time as we in ours. If they make any use of our writings it will be for their own ends, ends which we did not foresee, just as one picks up stones on the road and hurls them in the face of an aggressor. It would be quite vain on our part to throw off on them our effort to prolong our own existence: they have neither the duty nor the desire to do so. And since we have no means of acting upon these strangers, we shall present ourselves to them like beggars and beg them to lend us the appearance of life by using us for any purpose whatsoever. If we are Christians, we shall accept our lot humbly, provided only that they still speak of us, even though they use us to show that faith is ineffectual; if we are atheists, we shall be very happy if they still concern themselves with our anguish and our errors, were it even to prove that man is miserable without God. Would you be satisfied, Monsieur Schlumberger, if after the Revolution our grandsons saw in your writings the most obvious example of the conditioning of art by the economic structure? And if you do not have that literary destiny, you will have another that will be hardly any better: if you escape from dialectical materialism, it will be perhaps to serve the ends of some sort of psychoanalysis. In any case, our grandchildren will be impudent orphans, so why should we concern ourselves with them? Perhaps of all of us, only Céline will endure; it is theoretically possible, although highly improbable, that the twenty-first century will remember Drieu's name and forget Malraux's; in any case it will not espouse our quarrels, it will not mention what today we call the betrayal of certain writers; or if it mentions this, it will do so without anger or contempt. But what difference does it make to us? What Malraux and Drieu are for us is an absolute. In certain hearts there is an absolute of contempt for Drieu and an absolute of friendship for Malraux that one hundred posthumous judgments will not be able to shake. There is a living Malraux, a lump of warm blood in the very heart of our time, and there will be a dead Malraux at the mercy of history. Why should the living man try to fix the image of the dead man he will one day be? Certainly he lives beyond himself; his gaze and his concerns go beyond the death of his flesh; the *presence* of a man and his weight are measured not by the fifty or sixty years of his organic life, nor by the borrowed life he will lead in future centuries in the minds of strangers: they are measured by his own choice of the temporal cause that goes beyond him. The story is told that the runner of Marathon was dead an hour before he reached Athens. He was dead, yet he still ran; he ran dead and as a dead man announced the victory of the Greeks. It is a beautiful myth and shows that the dead act for a little while as if they were still alive. A little while—one year, ten years, fifty years perhaps, in any case, a *finite* period; and then they are buried for the second time. This is the measure that we propose to the writer: as long as his books provoke anger, embarrassment, shame, hatred, love, he will live, even if he is only a shadow. After that, the deluge. We are for a finite morality and a finite art.

A Note on The Visit of the Old Lady

FRIEDRICH DUERRENMATT

The Visit of the Old Lady is a story which takes place in a small town anywhere in central Europe, a story written by a person who is in no way remote from these people and who is not so sure that he would act any differently. Whatever more the story is needs neither to be said here nor staged in the theatre. This holds true for the conclusion as well. To be sure, the people speak more solemnly here than would be natural in reality, somewhat more in the direction of what is called "literature" or "elevated speech," but only because the people of Güllen have now become wealthy and, as *nouveaux riches,* speak more carefully too. I describe human beings, not marionettes, an action, not an allegory; I set forth a world, not a moral as is from time to time attributed to me. In fact, I do not even attempt to confront my play with the world, because all of this naturally comes to pass of itself, as long as the public forms a part of the theatre. For me, a theatrical piece is played within the possibilities of the stage, not in the garb of any style. When the men of Güllen play the parts of trees, it is not for the sake of surrealism but in order to move the somewhat painful love story which is taking place in this forest—namely, the attempt of an old man to come near to an old lady—into a poetic stage area and thus render it bearable. I write out of an inherent faith in the theatre and in the actor. This is my main motivating force. The material intrigues me. The actor needs but little to represent a man: only the outermost skin, the text, which of course must be right. I mean: just the way an organism closes itself off by forming a skin—an outside limit, a theatrical piece closes itself off by means

Friedrich Duerrenmatt, *"Der Besuch der alten Dame:* Anmerkung," *Komödien* I, Peter Schifferli Verlags AG, Zürich, 1957, pp. 357-359. Translated by Herman Salinger.

of language. The playwright gives this alone. Language is his result. For this reason one cannot work at language in itself, but only at that which makes language, at the thought, perhaps at the action; only dilettantes work at the language itself, at the style itself. The task of the actor consists, I believe, in attempting to achieve this result anew: what is art must now appear as nature. Let the foreground which I give be played correctly, the background will put in its appearance of itself. I do not count myself among the *avant-garde* of today; to be sure, I, too, have a theory of art—anything for the sake of amusement—but I withhold it as my private opinion (otherwise I should have to act in accordance with it) and prefer to be considered a somewhat confused primitive with an inadequate sense of form. The staging of my work should be in the direction of the folk drama; if they treat me as a sort of conscious Nestroy, they will get along best. Let them stick to my flashes of thought and forget the profundity, take care to have uninterrupted changes of scene without a curtain, play the automobile scene simply, preferably with a stage car on which only those things necessary for the performance are mounted: car seat, steering wheel, bumper. The automobile should be seen from the front with the rear seats raised; all of this must, of course, be new, as new as the yellow shoes, etc. (This scene has nothing to do with Wilder—why? Dialectical exercise for critics.) Claire Zachanassian represents neither justice nor the Marshall Plan nor even the Apocalypse; let her be only what she is: the richest woman in the world, whose fortune has put her in a position to act like the heroine of a Greek tragedy: absolute, cruel, something like Medea. She can afford it. The lady has a sense of humor—this must not be overlooked—since she keeps her distance from people as from purchasable goods, distance also from herself. She preserves a strange grace; moreover, a malicious charm. But since she moves outside of the human order, she has become something immutable, rigid, without any further development, unless it be that of petrification into a stone idol. She is a poetic apparition—likewise her retinue, even the eunuchs, who are not to be portrayed with unappetizing realism and with castrated voices but, on the contrary, as unreal, legendary, gentle, ghostly in their vegetative happiness, victims of a total revenge as logical as the law books of ancient times. (To make the roles easier, the pair can also speak alternately instead of in unison, but then without repetition of sentences.) If Claire Zachanassian is unmoved, a heroine from the beginning, her old lover must grow into a hero. A small tradesman gone to seed, he unsuspectingly falls victim to her in the beginning; guilty, he is of the opinion that life has automatically wiped out all guilt, an unthinking male, a simple man upon whom an idea dawns slowly, through fear, through terror, through something highly personal, who experiences justice in his own case because he recognizes his guilt, who becomes great through his dying (his death should not lack a certain monumentality). His death is at once meaningful and meaningless. It could only be meaningful in the mythical realm of an antique city-state, whereas the story takes places in Güllen. In the present. In addition to the hero and heroine there are the people of Güllen, human beings like all of us. They are not to be portrayed as evil, certainly not; at first resolved to reject the offer, they now contract debts, yet not with the intention of killing Ill but merely out of frivolity, out of a feeling that everything can be arranged all right. This is the way the Second Act should be staged—also the scene at the railway station, in which fear is experienced by Ill alone, who grasps his situation; as yet no angry word has been spoken. Not until the scene in the Peters' barn does the turning point come. Doom is no longer to be avoided. From now on the people of Güllen prepare themselves gradually for the murder, become outraged over Ill's guilt, and so on. Only his family deludes itself until the end that everything will turn out all right; they too are not evil, only weak, like all of us. It is a community which slowly gives in to temptation, like the teacher, but this yielding must be understandable. The temptation is too great, the poverty too bitter. *The Visit of the Old Lady* is a wicked play, yet for this very reason it must not be presented wickedly, but most humanely, with sadness, not with anger, but also with humor, for nothing harms this comedy —which ends tragically—more than brutal seriousness.